Civic Education at a Crossroads

This book turns to political theory as a framework for understanding the rise of political and religious extremism, and in particular the Christian Nationalist position, identifying solutions to civic challenges, and arguing for the vital role that public schools play in providing the civic education that prepares young people for participation in democratic self-government.

Drawing on scholarly debates between liberal and republican political theorists, the author maintains that if we want to preserve our republic, then policymakers and educators must unapologetically promote a normative "vision of good citizenship" that cultivates in students the requisite civic virtue and rational autonomy needed to defend democracy from the rise of illiberal extremism.

Providing a timely contribution to academic debates about the role of civic education in the preservation of democracy, it will appeal to scholars, educators, and policymakers concerned with the future of civic education, as well as the philosophy of education, political science, and educational policy.

Bryan J. Henry is Professor of Political Science at Lone Star College, the United States.

Routledge Research in Character and Virtue Education

This series provides a forum for established and emerging scholars to discuss the latest debates, research and theory relating to virtue education, character education and value education.

Virtues and Virtue Education in Theory and Practice
Are Virtues Local or Universal?
Catherine A. Darnell and Kristján Kristjánsson

A Christian Education in the Virtues
Character Formation and Human Flourishing
James Arthur

Seven Democratic Virtues of Liberal Education
A Student-Inspired Agenda for Teaching Civic Virtue in European Universities
Teun J. Dekker

Historical and Contemporary Foundations of Social Studies Education
Unpacking Implications for Civic Education and Contemporary Life
James E. Schul

Ubuntu Virtue Theory and Moral Character Formation
Critically Reconstructing Ubuntu for the African Educational Context
Grivas Muchineripi Kayange

Civic Education at a Crossroads
The Christian Nationalist Threat to Public Schools
Bryan J. Henry

For more information about this series, please visit: www.routledge.com/Routledge-Research-in-Character-and-Virtue-Education/book-series/RRCVE

Civic Education at a Crossroads
The Christian Nationalist Threat
to Public Schools

Bryan J. Henry

NEW YORK AND LONDON

First published 2024
by Routledge
605 Third Avenue, New York, NY 10158

and by Routledge
4 Park Square, Milton Park, Abingdon, Oxon, OX14 4RN

Routledge is an imprint of the Taylor & Francis Group, an informa business

© 2024 Bryan J. Henry

The right of Bryan J. Henry to be identified as author of this work has been asserted in accordance with sections 77 and 78 of the Copyright, Designs and Patents Act 1988.

All rights reserved. No part of this book may be reprinted or reproduced or utilised in any form or by any electronic, mechanical, or other means, now known or hereafter invented, including photocopying and recording, or in any information storage or retrieval system, without permission in writing from the publishers.

Trademark notice: Product or corporate names may be trademarks or registered trademarks, and are used only for identification and explanation without intent to infringe.

Library of Congress Cataloging-in-Publication Data
Names: Henry, Bryan J., author.
Title: Civic education at a crossroads : the christian nationalist threat to public schools / Bryan J. Henry.
Description: New York, NY : Routledge, 2024. | Series: Routledge research in character and virtue education | Includes bibliographical references and index.
Identifiers: LCCN 2024001203 (print) | LCCN 2024001204 (ebook) | ISBN 9781032686035 (hardback) | ISBN 9781032686042 (paperback) | ISBN 9781032686059 (ebook)
Subjects: LCSH: Civics—Study and teaching—United States. | Nationalism—Religious aspects—Christianity. | Citizenship—Religious aspects—Christianity. | Political science—United States—Philosophy. | Religion in the public schools—United States.
Classification: LCC LC1091 .H366 2024 (print) | LCC LC1091 (ebook) | DDC 370.11/5—dc23/eng/20240125
LC record available at https://lccn.loc.gov/2024001203
LC ebook record available at https://lccn.loc.gov/2024001204

ISBN: 9781032686035 (hbk)
ISBN: 9781032686042 (pbk)
ISBN: 9781032686059 (ebk)

DOI: 10.4324/9781032686059

Typeset in Times New Roman
by Apex CoVantage, LLC

For Madeleine, Olivia, and Emerson

Contents

Epigraph   *ix*
Preface   *x*
Acknowledgments   *xi*

1 Civic Education at a Crossroads   1

Public Schools Cannot Remain Neutral on Democracy 1
The Christian Nationalist Threat to Public Schools 5
Watching Liberal Democracy Become a Partisan Issue 7
A Brief Note on Terminology 11

2 Quick, Someone Call a Political Theorist!   13

Democracy or Republic? 13
Political Theory to the Rescue? 17
Liberal Democracy Requires Republican Civic Virtue 20
Freedom, Civic Duty, and Public Health 22
A Case of Partisan Neutrality 25
Takeaways for Elected Officials and School
   Administrators 28

3 Moving From Neutral to Normative   30

Imagining a Normative Civic Education 30
Rational Autonomy and Civic Virtue 32
Diversity, Equity, and Inclusion, Oh My! 37
Christian Nationalism Infiltrates Suburban Houston 40
News of Christian Nationalism Spreads Across Texas 43
Takeaways for Students and Parents 45

4 The Root of the Problem   48

Liberal Democracy's Neutrality 48
Teaching Lies to Teach the Truth 51
From Teaching Both Sides to Picking Sides 54
Laboratories of Christian Nationalism 58
Takeaways for Educators 60

5 A Republic, If We Teach It   62

The Perfectionist Rationale for Civic Education 62
Revolutionary and Illiberal Conservatism 66
Minority Tyranny and Liberal Democracy 68
Civic Reformation 71

Index   76

Epigraph

Fundamentalists rush in where liberals fear to tread.

—Michael J. Sandel

Preface

The basic premise of this book formed during my encounter with various "critics of liberalism" in my graduate studies in political theory at The University of Houston. The conversation between liberal, republican, and communitarian political theorists fascinated me, and I often grappled with their ideas within the context of my own professional identity as a civic educator.

For me, providing a meaningful civic education in the hyper-partisan environment of the United States has proven challenging. I have witnessed fellow educators neglect or abandon civic education and have myself experienced aggressive hostility to civic education by those opposed to the civic mission of public schools. I am often torn between a critical focus on America's inadequacies and failure to live up to its values and a deep reverence and pride toward its accomplishments, ideals, and aspirations.

As I see the United States increasingly divided along partisan lines, and threatened by ideologies at odds with liberal democracy, my hope is that *Civic Education at a Crossroads* can contribute something useful toward a solution to our civic crisis. If elected officials and educators are inspired to defend and promote the principles of liberal democracy, both to preserve the American republic and to ensure that the next generation enjoys a democratic way of life, then I will consider this work a success.

Acknowledgments

I wish to express my sincere gratitude to the individuals who sparked my interest in political theory and facilitated my exploration of deep questions about how to live.

My introduction to political theory occurred at Texas A&M University, and I will never forget the initial excitement and sense of possibility experienced in my undergraduate coursework with Scott Austin, Kristi Sweet, and Theodore George.

My graduate work in political theory at The University of Houston was shepherded by Jeffrey Church, and I am grateful for the countless hours of conversation and mentoring that he so willingly provided.

I also wish to thank my parents for modeling the joy of reading and providing me the space and support to chart my own educational and professional path.

Lastly, my wife Brittany has provided me both the professional and personal support without which I could not have completed this project. Her love, encouragement, and resilience inspire me.

1 Civic Education at a Crossroads

Public Schools Cannot Remain Neutral on Democracy

When Vice President-elect Mike Pence attended the Broadway production of *Hamilton* shortly after the 2016 election, the cast made a direct appeal to him after the show, stating, "We truly hope that this show has inspired you to uphold our American values and work on behalf of *all* of us."[1] While this plea was intended more as an affirmation of diversity than a call to preserve the integrity of democratic self-government, Pence nonetheless decided to uphold the U.S. Constitution four years later, when under enormous pressure from Donald Trump to exercise unprecedented authority during the certification of the Electoral College vote, he refused to do so and upheld the rule of law. Did he honor his oath to the U.S. Constitution because of that night at the theater in New York City? Doubtful, but it does highlight one of the central questions being asked by civic educators across the United States, especially since the January 6th Insurrection and the rise of Christian Nationalism: how should public schools teach the beliefs and behaviors of liberal democracy and how can we produce citizens committed to the values of our diverse, pluralistic republic?

Is it possible to identify the characteristics of good citizenship? If so, does that necessarily mean it is appropriate for the government, through the public school system, to promote a normative "vision of good citizenship"? While some might assume it is self-evident, given its historical origins, that providing civic education is one of the most basic responsibilities of the public school system, others might argue that it is too difficult to agree on a shared definition of good citizenship, and therefore, schools should stick to a description of the mechanics of how government works without committing to value judgments about how people ought to conduct themselves when participating in politics.

In today's hyper-partisan political climate, one may hear an angry parent at a school board meeting make a version of this argument by stating, "stick to the basics of writing, reading, and math and let the parents handle values."

After all, as some political theorists have observed, a liberal democracy like the United States tends to value individual freedom and personal choice above all else, so how can public schools justify telling young people how they ought to approach their civic life? Some might insist that promoting a normative "vision of good citizenship," that is, telling students how they *ought* to approach the role of citizen, is going beyond what is appropriate. Today, we hear urgent calls to respect "parental rights" or "bring God back into the schools," but which parents and whose God should determine how public schools prepare students for their civic obligations and opportunities?

As a civic educator myself for the last 14 years, I have come to the conviction that the preservation of America's constitutional republic requires that public schools unapologetically promote a normative civic education that boldly endorses a "vision of good citizenship" that takes sides on what is right and wrong. While I agree that the government should not endorse what political theorists call a "vision of the good life,"[2] that is, telling people how they should live in a comprehensive sense, I believe that in the context of civic education, especially in this historical moment, it is appropriate and imperative that public schools promote a "vision of good citizenship." The truth is that good citizenship *can* be defined, and Americans agree that democratic self-government in a republic is the best form of government and means to individual and collective well-being. America's public schools should teach students why this is the case and prepare them to preserve their democratic way of life and republican form of government.

A liberal democracy can only perpetuate itself if it deliberately produces citizens who are able and willing to live out the beliefs and behaviors necessary to do so. American society has become so culturally divided and politically polarized that most public schools have attempted to maintain neutrality or achieve some sort of apolitical identity. The motivations are varied: avoiding the complaints of parents, or worse, charges of "indoctrination"; prioritizing subject matter that is assessed on standardized tests, which results in a deficient civic education; or fearing expensive legal challenges for violating a restrictive state law. The result is the gradual development and acceptance of illiberal, undemocratic, and authoritarian beliefs and behaviors throughout American society. Why should the public school system be prevented from performing one of its fundamental civic tasks during a time of civic crisis? If one of the public school's basic responsibilities is civic education, then why do we not look to it for civic renewal? Furthermore, why are some attacking and undermining the civic mission of public schools?

Try to imagine a Christian church that was prevented from preaching the tenets of its faith. Imagine the leaders of the church telling themselves, "It would be inappropriate to teach the next generation to carry on our values, practices, traditions, and norms because it might offend those who do not believe in Christianity." Imagine the members of the church acquiescing to claims that it would be "indoctrination" to cultivate a commitment to certain beliefs and behaviors. It is almost impossible to conjure this image because it is entirely contrary to the purpose of the church and its self-preservation. Why then, do we expect public schools in a republic to stay silent, or somehow "neutral," about the benefits of a democratic way of life and the personal beliefs and behaviors necessary for citizens to preserve it? Why do we leave the health and fate of our democracy up to chance? To me, it seems obvious that a democratic republic should aim to intentionally produce individuals committed to the political ideals and civic obligations that would preserve itself.

Furthermore, promoting the beliefs and behaviors of liberal democracy is about more than just the health or preservation of the political system; it is about our quality of life as individuals who interact with others within a community. Pluralism, tolerance, freedom of expression, and many other characteristics of liberal society are threatened by the rise of authoritarian and illiberal movements. One challenge that political theorists have identified with endorsing a normative civic education is that it may involve the promotion of specific values, which could be incompatible with notions of individual autonomy and "parental rights."[3] Yet public schools teach values every day when they discourage drug use and bullying, so why should it be controversial to encourage the values and behaviors necessary to preserve a democratic society from authoritarian threats?

Americans inhabit a historical moment where a violent mob of insurrectionists, many carrying Christian Nationalist messages and symbols, tried to overthrow the government. A different sort of mob, also inspired by Christian Nationalism, is attempting to hijack the civic mission of public schools. Illiberalism is on the offensive, whether it is at the U.S. Capitol, statehouses across the country or at school board meetings. At all levels of government, Christian Nationalists are attempting to use public institutions to undermine our democratic way of life. If preparing young Americans to preserve our republic in the face of these threats means promoting specific values, or making normative claims about what is right and wrong, then so be it.

For example, Americans do not believe in teaching intolerance or discrimination, so why do public schools stop short of positively promoting the values of tolerance and inclusivity? Why should public schools remain neutral? If a multicultural, pluralistic republic like the United States requires tolerance, then public schools should endorse tolerance as a desirable, good, and healthy value. Likewise, our society does not believe in authoritarian systems of government. Americans do not believe that the political systems in China or Iran are equally valid options to their own, so why do civic educators hesitate to identify authoritarian behavior and actively denounce it? Why should it be controversial for a teacher to criticize political statements or actions that are, by definition, anti-democratic and authoritarian? In other words, does it make sense for the public schools in a democracy to remain neutral on democracy itself?

Recently, critics claiming the mantle of "parental rights" have been vocal in opposing the role that public schools play in shaping the values of their children, insisting that parents, not schools, should decide what their children learn. While it goes without saying that parents have a significant role to play in their child's education, it harms the health of our republic for parents to undermine the civic mission of public schools by opposing programs that promote tolerance, empathy, and critical thinking. Parents who insist that schools are "indoctrinating" students simply because they promote inclusivity and tolerance toward the LGBTQ+ community are actively undermining the political and civic equality at the heart of a liberal society.

Public schools exist to prepare young people for participation in the workforce and political process. A family can believe whatever they want about LGBTQ+ rights in the privacy of their home or church, and parents can teach their children whatever they want based on their personal views or faith, but public schools should be able to promote the beliefs and behaviors that are necessary for the maintenance of inclusive workplaces and public policies that provide equal protection for everyone under the law. Parents should not be able to limit the ability of a public school to teach tolerance simply because it contradicts their personal intolerance.

A parent opposed to the promotion of inclusivity for the LGBTQ+ community may argue that it violates their religious liberty, but the purpose of the public school system is not to reinforce each family's personal or religious values. Some parents may interpret their faith in a way that denies the LGBTQ+ community their dignity and equality, while other parents may interpret their faith in a way that affirms and celebrates the LGBTQ+ community. To allow one group of parents to silence public schools based on the notion that the "government" is teaching values or beliefs that contradict their religion is not a defense of religious liberty; it is a violation of the civic mission of public schools by religion.

The government does not tell people of faith what to preach at church or interfere with their transmission of values, and people of faith, even if they happen to be a local majority, should not be able to tell public schools what they can teach or prevent them from providing the civic education necessary for participation in a diverse, pluralistic society. Furthermore, public schools are not simply preparing young people for the diversity they will encounter in society and the workforce; they are also tasked with providing a civic education that prepares students for participation in the political process. A meaningful civic education should promote the values, beliefs, and behaviors that are necessary for the preservation of democratic self-government. Parents should not be able to prevent public schools from teaching the values and skills of democracy simply because they have embraced authoritarian tendencies or succumbed to illiberal inclinations. Yet that is exactly what is happening across the United States, especially in Texas where I live and teach.

The Christian Nationalist Threat to Public Schools

The civic mission of the public school system is under aggressive assault. Consider the following examples just from the Lone Star State:

- The Texas legislature passed a bill, HB 3979, to prevent an accurate teaching of American history by preventing educators from fully discussing the topics of slavery, white supremacy, racial discrimination, and systemic racism. The same bill requires teachers to teach "both sides" of any controversial or contemporary political issue. The result has been a reluctance to teach how much progress has been made to overcome the historical legacy of discrimination and actively ignoring the injustices that still exist today.[4]
- The Texas Education Agency, the governor, and other elected officials created an atmosphere of anxiety and intimidation by labeling books that discuss sexual orientation or gender identity as "pornographic" and in need of review. The result has been the removal of many books from school libraries and the return of a more hostile school atmosphere for LGBTQ+ youth.[5]
- The Texas legislature passed a law mandating that all public schools display signs with the national motto "In God We Trust" if donated. In northwest Houston, where such signs were delivered to every campus in one of the state's largest school districts, those who paid for them celebrated on social media that the signs "allow us to have God and country placed back into the halls of learning as our Founding Fathers intended."[6] The Texas legislature tried, but failed, to pass a law requiring that the Ten Commandments be displayed in each classroom.

Similar developments have occurred across the United States. The source of this attack on the civic mission of public schools is a faction of political and religious extremists motivated by what scholars now label "Christian Nationalism." Andrew Whitehead and Samuel Perry, the authors of *Taking America Back for God: Christian Nationalism in the United States*, define it as "an ideology that idealizes and advocates a fusion of American civic life with a particular type of Christian identity and culture."[7] Christian Nationalists often seem to believe that they are saving America from progressive and secular forces and restoring it to its Christian roots. Furthermore, they typically express deep reverence for the U.S. Constitution, but their actions and expressed beliefs are often completely at odds with the principles of the American Founding, such as religious pluralism.

Christian Nationalism, according to Whitehead and Perry's data, "includes assumptions of nativism, white supremacy, patriarchy, and heteronormativity, along with divine sanction for authoritarian control and militarism."[8] Seen in this light, I argue that it is evident that Christian Nationalism is the common source of all the seemingly disparate attacks on public schools and education professionals. In the same spirit that Whitehead and Perry insist we cannot understand the divides within American politics without an understanding of Christian Nationalism, I contend that we cannot understand the recent and ongoing illiberal assault on the civic mission of public schools without recognizing that Christian Nationalism is the ideology fueling all of it. In other words, Christian Nationalism is the thread connecting opposition to face masks during a pandemic, classroom discussions about racism, and novels about the LGBTQ+ community.

In *The Flag and the Cross: White Christian Nationalism and the Threat to American Democracy*, another book by Samuel Perry, co-authored with Philip Gorski, they argue that Christian Nationalism is a worldview that "includes cherished assumptions about what America was and is, but also what it *should be*."[9] In other words, Christian Nationalism contains within it normative aspirations regarding American identity, and those motivated by it will necessarily promote a normative vision, or make normative claims, about American society. If it is true, as Perry and Gorski argue, that "the United States cannot be both a truly multiracial democracy . . . and a white Christian nation at the same time,"[10] then we must contend with the reality that Christian Nationalists have chosen to pursue their preference for the latter and intend to use the public school system, or at least public tax dollars, as a means to that end. In other words, if Christian Nationalists have abandoned pluralism and the "neutrality" of a liberal society, then those who want to preserve and perfect multiracial democracy must pick sides too.

After they invaded the U.S. Capitol and failed to overturn the results of a presidential election, Christian Nationalists began invading school board meetings across the country to denounce the progressive, liberal, and "woke" agenda that they insist public schools are imposing on American students. Such "wokeism" includes not only the history of white supremacy and the promotion of equality for the LGBTQ+ community but also any aspect of the curriculum that teaches values and behaviors that are incompatible with or problematic for their undemocratic and authoritarian movement. They would insist that a social studies teacher who describes the events of January 6, 2021 as an insurrection is guilty of political bias and indoctrination, but not doing so is to normalize political violence as an acceptable form of behavior. For example, to comply with HB 3979 in Texas and present "both sides" of the issue would require the teacher to ask students to consider whether the actions of the rioters were "patriotic" instead. If public schools are unable to clearly state that attempts to violently overthrow the government after losing an election are wrong, antidemocratic, and un-American, then their civic mission has been hijacked by those who clearly lack an authentic allegiance to liberal democracy.

Perry and Gorski discuss working against an illiberal triumph by the forces of Christian Nationalism largely in political terms, claiming that "the only way to avert that outcome is to build a popular front in defense of American democracy,"[11] but they do not discuss education or the role of public schools in this strategy. It is vital that defenders of American democracy recognize the role that public schools and civic education play in the preservation of republican self-government. Clearly, the multi-pronged assault on the civic mission of public schools is evidence enough that Christian Nationalists believe that public schools are a major battlefield in the war for America's identity. Political coalitions that unite Republicans and Democrats to defeat illiberal candidates at the ballot box will be futile if Christian Nationalists occupy the K-12 public school system and produce young people who are primed to affirm Christian Nationalist rhetoric and priorities.

Toward the end of their book, Perry and Gorski claim that "America is at a crossroads."[12] I wholeheartedly agree, but I believe that crossroads is located within our public schools. It is more necessary, and justified, than ever for public schools to defend the values of a shared democratic way of life and cultivate within young people the beliefs and behaviors necessary to preserve democratic self-government. *Civic education* is at a crossroads. For American public schools to sit on the sidelines in adherence to liberal "neutrality," while Christian Nationalists proudly go on the offensive, is a recipe for civic disaster.

Watching Liberal Democracy Become a Partisan Issue

Within the current political climate, individuals or organizations that promote the values of liberal democracy are now often accused of being "political" or having an "agenda." This is the same argument that many "parental rights" groups are making about public schools when they object to literature that depicts same-sex relationships, history lessons that teach the legacy of white supremacy, or social-emotional learning programs that encourage inclusion for the LGBTQ+ community. To some, it may seem unwise or unfathomable for public schools, in such a political climate, to double down on the promotion of democratic values, but that is exactly what needs to be done. No longer content to promote their worldview in their homes, churches, or private schools, Christian Nationalists are now demanding that the public school system reflect their values too. These political and religious extremists claim to be against indoctrination, but they are trying to use public schools to impose an agenda at odds with the diversity and pluralism of American society. According to Perry and Gorski, "Christian nationalists believe that America should be a Christian nation, or, at least, a nation ruled by Christians."[13]

As an educator, activist, and parent, I have experienced and witnessed the gradual rise of Christian Nationalism firsthand. My teaching career started in 2011, during Obama's presidency, in an affluent and conservative suburb of northeast Houston. I experienced the rise of the Tea Party, which is now understood to have had major Christian Nationalist undercurrents, and the impact it had on education issues. For example, the 2012 party platform for the Texas GOP formally expressed opposition to the teaching of "critical thinking" on the grounds that it undermined parental authority. As a high school social studies teacher, I personally experienced the scrutiny and pushback that can come from conservative parents if their children are equipped to think for themselves about politics or current events. I witnessed the reluctance of administrators to support teachers when they sought to teach the truth or tackle contemporary issues. All of this was *before* Donald Trump became president.

To be a social studies teacher during and after the 2016 presidential election was intense. In my case, I witnessed a dramatic change overnight in terms of the microscope that my teaching was under. Conservative parents were aggressive in rooting out anyone who dared to speak critically about Trump and his actions either as a candidate or as president. Where it might have been common for a teacher to discuss Barack Obama, or even criticize his actions, it was now "political" to discuss Donald Trump at all. The fall of 2016 was a turning point for me not just as a teacher but also as a student. I completed my M.A. in political science after five years as a part-time student and full-time teacher. I had applied to graduate school back in 2011 during my first year in the classroom after I was laid off due to state budget cuts during the Great Recession. Now, in 2016, I was teaching AP U.S. Government, making annual trips to Washington, DC with my students, and writing freelance political commentary for the local newspaper.

In 2019, I had the opportunity to transition to higher education at a local community college. I taught on-campus for one semester; then, the pandemic closed our campus, and I taught primarily online for the next few semesters. I experienced survivor's guilt as my colleagues in the K-12 system were forced back into the classroom under impossible circumstances. In Texas, schools were legally barred from requiring face masks during the pandemic. Teachers and parents who promoted face masks were denounced by those who viewed public health recommendations as a form of tyranny. Then, the same people who were outraged about face masks started yelling about Critical Race Theory (CRT). Then, they started yelling about "pornography" in the school libraries. Long story short, I know that I would not have made it had I been in the secondary classroom the last few years. I would have quit in protest, been fired for insubordination, or literally chased out of the building by angry parents. I still remember the trauma of teaching American government to confused and angry teenagers the day after Trump's election. I cannot imagine how I would have handled the events of January 6, 2021.

As I witnessed all the insanity that was engulfing the public school system, I resolved to be a voice for the teachers who were too scared or too exhausted to speak up for themselves. I started attending school board meetings and networking with other concerned parents and educators. As I watched each new wave of ignorance and vitriol crash into our public schools, I was constantly recalling what I had studied in graduate school and started to analyze each troubling event through the lens of political theory. Why are people so opposed to face masks? Why are religious extremists under the impression that public schools should not teach anything that is incompatible with their faith? Why are school boards failing to stand up to people who are clearly racist and homophobic? For me, my academic background in political theory offered a framework for understanding what was happening and identifying solutions to our civic crisis. An understanding of Christian Nationalism, while necessary and useful for putting the different pieces of the problem together, does not provide a path forward or a constructive alternative.

The question that I kept asking myself, which took me back to my graduate studies and experience as a high school teacher, was how public schools can promote the type of normative civic education that is necessary for the preservation of the American republic and renewal of its democratic way of life. Political and religious extremists accusing public schools of indoctrination is not new, but in the past, this minority that we now call Christian Nationalists would have chosen to home school or send their children to private Christian schools. Now, the civic mission of the public school system is under assault by those who want to conquer it and use it to impose their values and agenda on everyone else. And, if it is not troubling enough that their main focus seems to be hindering or preventing any discussion or instruction about race and sexual orientation, their basic commitment to liberal democracy itself is also now in doubt.

Like those who use their free speech to spread misinformation about "stolen" elections on social media, those who are attacking public schools are using the infrastructure of America's democratic society to undermine it. Christian Nationalists are investing heavily in school board elections to subvert the civic mission of public schools from the inside. As Steven Levitsky and Daniel Ziblatt, the authors of *How Democracies Die*, have observed, "the tragic paradox of the electoral route to authoritarianism is that democracy's assassins use the very institutions of democracy—gradually, subtly, and even legally—to kill it."[14] Americans must not allow those opposed to the values of a diverse, pluralistic republic to hijack and corrupt the civic mission of the public school system that prepares young people for political participation. Christian Nationalists are mobilizing to impose their worldview on society by taking over public schools. To save public education, and the republic itself, Americans must resolve to fight back and defend its democratic way of life.

In Texas, where one out of every ten American children goes to school, Christian Nationalists are taking control of school boards one by one. Policymakers and administrators can no longer avoid being accused of "politics" by those who now see what is good for democracy as "indoctrination" by Democrats. Educators and parents can no longer avoid accusations of "partisanship" by those who object to preparing students for democracy in a diverse, pluralistic republic. Americans who cherish the principles of liberal democracy have no control over the fact that an extremist faction within the Republican Party and conservative movement has embraced an anti-democratic, Christian Nationalist worldview. For too long, the mainstream media has been unwilling to call out the illiberal threat to democracy due to fear and a desire to be "neutral" between the two parties. The result has been the normalization of anti-democratic ideas and behaviors.

The threat to the public school system is *more* dangerous than the partisanship that has undermined American media. Again, no longer content to have their own private schools promote their worldview, Christian Nationalists are now trying to take over public schools too. Imagine if Fox News was trying to take over PBS or control how networks like NBC or ABC report the news. Imagine if PBS wasn't allowed to identify a lie as a lie because it might offend those viewers who believe the lie. That is what is at stake right now with American public education. Our schools may soon be unable to call a violent insurrection that attempted to prevent the peaceful transfer of power after a free and fair election what it was because it might offend the insurrectionists and their sympathizers. This has escalated beyond the familiar "Culture War" disagreements over sex education and LGBTQ+ equality. This is about the preservation of American democracy and a democratic way of life.

My hope is to use my knowledge of political theory and experience as a classroom teacher to increase an understanding of what is at stake right now and offer a vision of how we can move forward and continue the intergenerational project of gradually perfecting our Union. In my graduate research, I focused much of my attention on political theorists referred to as "critics of liberalism" and I applied their academic debates to the context of civic education in public schools. This book will provide a survey of liberal and republican ideas about the role of government and civic education and then apply them to current events I have experienced or witnessed in suburban school districts in Houston, Texas.

The genesis for the book's claim that public schools should unapologetically promote a normative "vision of good citizenship" that prepares American youth for participation in a diverse, pluralistic republic lies in something I quickly perceived while teaching in a conservative suburb. There are too many parents who do not want their children to be taught "both sides" or "all angles" of an issue if doing so places their personal political or religious worldview on equal footing with alternatives. There are too many parents who do not want their children to think for themselves if doing so means they might adopt values at odds with those they have been taught at home. They deeply resent that their children meet educators who open their minds to diversity of thought.

As a high school teacher, and now as a college professor, I have always been committed to providing my students with a critical civic education that equips them to form their own political identity. I tell my students that they will probably leave my class just as liberal or conservative as when they entered it, but they should understand far more deeply their own political worldview and the political worldview of those they disagree with. I have been accused by some of having a bias, but the way I see it I simply don't have a conservative bias. What

I quickly learned teaching in a conservative suburb is that being "neutral" and teaching "both sides" will be perceived as having a bias *against* conservative values. Far too often, ideas that do not reinforce conservative values are perceived as an attack on them. The problem according to political and religious extremists, it seems, is not bias but the "wrong" bias. The Christian Nationalists legislating in statehouses and yelling at school board meetings across America claim to oppose a biased education with a "woke" agenda, but their misguided crusade to "save America" is threatening to impose a truly biased education with an agenda that may cause the demise of the American republic.

A Brief Note on Terminology

It is important to me to be clear, from the outset, about the meaning of the words I am using and the people I am talking about.

Christian Nationalists: As defined in Chapter 1, Christian Nationalists are individuals who adhere to specific assumptions and beliefs about America's identity. They are typically conservative Christians who vote for the Republican Party, but it is crucial to understand that plenty of conservative Christians and Republicans *reject* Christian Nationalism. Still, Christian Nationalists promote a conservative Christian agenda, so I will use the words Christian Nationalist and "conservative Christian" or "conservative Republican" interchangeably at times. In other words, I am only talking about *you* if I'm talking about you.

Liberal democracy and republican self-government: As defined in Chapter 2, liberal democracy is a system of government based on the principles of liberalism, which include an emphasis on limited government, individual rights, equal treatment and opportunity, freedom of speech, religious toleration and pluralism, checks and balances, and the rule of law. Republican self-government refers to the act of individuals participating in a representative government based on popular sovereignty. I will use the words liberal democracy and republican self-government interchangeably to refer to the principles and practices of the American republic, which the vast majority of Republicans and Democrats support despite their policy disagreements.

Private school/homeschool: Throughout the book, I will refer to private schools and homeschooling as sites where the ideology of Christian Nationalism is promoted and influential. I understand many private schools and homeschoolers do *not* promote Christian Nationalism, and my description of the role that private schools and homeschooling play in spreading Christian Nationalism is not intended to disparage the hard work of educators in those settings. Again, I'm only talking about *you* if I'm talking about you.

Notes

1. Caroline Framke, "Mike Pence Went to See Hamilton. The Audience Booed—But the Cast Delivered a Personal Plea," www.vox.com, November 19, 2016.
2. Michael Sandel, *Democracy's Discontent* (Cambridge: Harvard University Press, 1996), 4.
3. William Galston, "Two Concepts of Liberalism," *Ethics* 105, no. 3 (April 1995): 523.
4. Brian Lopez, "Republican Bill That Limits How Race, Slavery and History Are Taught in Texas Schools Becomes Law," December 2, 2021, www.texastribune.org.
5. Cassandra Pollock, "Gov. Greg Abbott Calls for Criminal Investigation Into Availability of Pornographic Books in Public Schools," November 10, 2021, www.texastribune.org.
6. Jason Miles, "In God We Trust Signs Mandatory in Texas Public Schools If Privately Donated," August 16, 2022, www.khou.com.
7. Andrew L. Whitehead and Samuel L. Perry, *Taking America Back for God: Christian Nationalism in the United States* (New York: Oxford University Press, 2020), xx.
8. Ibid., 10.
9. Philip S. Gorski and Samuel L. Perry, *The Flag and the Cross: White Christian Nationalism and the Threat to American Democracy* (New York: Oxford University Press, 2022), 3.
10. Ibid., 8.
11. Ibid., 11.
12. Ibid., 127.
13. Ibid., 6.
14. Steven Levitsky and Daniel Ziblatt, *How Democracies Die* (New York: Crown, 2018), 8–9.

2 Quick, Someone Call a Political Theorist!

Democracy or Republic?

The American Founding is rightfully described as "radical" because it involved the rejection of monarchy, aristocracy, and state religion. It is also accurately described as an "experiment" because it represented an attempt to form a republic unlike any that had ever existed before. Historically, republics were supposed to be small and worked well only with a homogenous population. As James Madison explained in *The Federalist*, the newly created American republic would be geographically large and contain a diverse array of factions. For Madison, and other Federalists, the size and diversity of the American republic would be assets that would help avoid the tyranny of a dominant faction. Whereas the Anti-Federalists, opposed to the ratification of a new federal constitution, warned that "history furnishes no example of a free republic, anything like the extent of the United States" and, furthermore, that "in a large republic, the public good is sacrificed to a thousand views,"[1] Madison insisted that the design of the new federal system would "secure the public good, and private rights, against the danger"[2] of a majority faction.

Madison made a distinction, in his mind, between a democracy and republic. A democracy was "a society consisting of a small number of citizens, who assemble and administer the government in person,"[3] while a republic was "a government in which the scheme of representation takes place."[4] Many Americans, taking their cue from Madison himself, continue to insist on a strong difference in meaning between the words democracy and republic and seem to believe that much is at stake if the United States is rightfully regarded as one or the other. My personal suspicion has always been that this is because our two major political parties happen to have these same words embedded in their names. Perhaps some Republicans believe that if the United States is a republic, then it will help their cause, and likewise, Democrats believe that their fortunes will be improved if the United States is a democracy. The truth is that these two words are interchangeable today. The United States is a constitutional republic, which means it is a representative democracy and I will use the terms interchangeably.

Today, those who see the United States as one of the world's greatest democracies often criticize the undemocratic elements of the American political system: for example, the use of the filibuster in the U.S. Senate to obstruct legislation supported by a large majority of the American public, or the fact that the Electoral College system can deny the presidency to the candidate who received the most votes from the American people. Increasingly, those who may agree (in theory) that these are objectionable aspects of the political process, but who benefit from them (in practice) because it helps their political party, evoke the fact that the United States is a republic as justification. The suggestion being, apparently, that a republic is somehow supposed to promote or allow minority rule. Some conservatives go so far as to deny that the United States is a democracy at all. For example, Senator Mike Lee of Utah tweeted during the 2020 election that "we're not a democracy"[5] and then clarified his tweet by stating that the United States is a constitutional republic. It seems the distinction that conservatives make between a democracy and republic is always intended as an explanation for why it is appropriate for the majority to be thwarted by the minority. However, as Madison explained, the expectation was that majority rule would be the norm in the American political system, but that the majority would be a coalition of minorities.

The minority rule that Republicans often enjoy when they exploit the countermajoritarian features of the American political system is something that Madison dismissed almost entirely, stating that "if a faction consists of less than a majority, relief is supplied by the republican principle, which enables the majority to defeat its sinister views, by regular vote."[6] Far from endorsing or expecting minority rule, Madison claimed that the majority could easily avoid control by a minority faction simply by outvoting them. As Madison understood it, the design of the new U.S. Constitution would easily prevent "tyranny of the minority," and he focused instead on the threat of majority factions, which he insisted were more likely to threaten the rights of the minority. So, while conservative Republicans may draw on the American Founding to justify their ability to block legislation as the minority or win elections with fewer votes, the Founders never imagined that a minority faction would be able to impose their values and agenda on a majority of the population. Yet a minority of Christian Nationalists imposing their beliefs on everyone else is exactly what threatens public schools across the United States today.

While the terms democracy and republic can be misunderstood or used to advance an agenda, political philosophies such as liberalism and republicanism also have a variety of historical meanings that differ from the partisan uses of the words today. The historical, or philosophical, meanings of liberalism and republicanism can illuminate much about the current challenges facing civic educators in public schools. For example, when introducing political philosophy to my students, I must remind them that liberalism does not necessarily have anything to do with Democrats or liberals today. Likewise, republicanism does not necessarily refer to anything that conservatives or Republicans believe or promote. I use the words democracy and republic interchangeably when referring to the American political system in the classroom, but I gravitate strongly toward the word republic because it implies the political philosophy of republicanism, which emphasizes active participation in politics, an obligation to seek the common good of society, and the exercise of civic virtue.

Republicanism has a long tradition dating back to ancient Greece and philosophers like Aristotle, who insisted that human beings could only realize their full potential by participating in collective self-government. Republicanism encourages civic virtue, which is "the ability of an individual to rise above personal or class interest to place the good of the whole community above one's own."[7] It is not hard to see why civic educators would be drawn to such a vision of citizenship. It also is not hard to see why Founders like James Madison and Thomas Jefferson were also inspired by the ideals of republicanism. As previously stated, the American Founding was a "radical experiment" in republicanism, in the notion that individuals could govern themselves both individually and collectively, that citizens could transcend their own narrow self-interest to identify and pursue the general welfare of society. Madison argued that the republican system being proposed by the U.S. Constitution would, in fact, make it more likely that the people's representatives could transcend the self-interest of factions to pursue the public good.

Yet, as inspirational, and aspirational as republican ideals may be, the American Founding and the U.S. Constitution were equally, if not more, influenced by another political philosophy: liberalism. Whereas republicanism asked the individual to pursue the common good, liberalism placed individual rights and freedom at the center of politics. Liberalism, unlike republicanism, was a new set of ideas coming out of the European Enlightenment. Liberal theorists like John Locke attempted to provide new answers to questions about the origin and purpose of government. In doing so, these liberal theorists offered new ideas about where government's power comes from and how government's power should be used. Locke famously described a "state of nature" prior to the existence of government wherein individuals possessed natural rights, that is, rights prior to government. For Locke, these natural rights that human beings automatically possessed included life, liberty, and property. The problem, said Locke, was that these natural rights were insecure in the "state of nature" because everyone was free to violate other people's rights.

The creation of government, what is referred to as the "social contract," takes place when the individuals in the "state of nature" decide collectively to give up some of their freedom in exchange for security. Government and law are created to provide the predictability and security necessary to exercise rights. The radical aspect of Locke's description is the implication that if the government was created by the people themselves for the purpose of protecting the natural rights they already possess, then government's power is limited to what the people have consented to give to it. Locke's ideas are, in many respects, the birth of the idea that government's power should be limited for the purpose of protecting individual rights. Furthermore, if the government was created to protect the rights of the individual, then the individual is entitled to question how government is using its power.

Thomas Jefferson famously employed this "social contract" theory when justifying the American rebellion against George III, insisting that when government ceases to protect individual rights, "it is the right of the people to alter or abolish it."[8] This emphasis on limiting government's power in the name of protecting individual liberty can result in liberalism emphasizing individualism more than community or the common good, placing it at odds with the vision of citizenship promoted by republicanism. If the ideals of republicanism are disregarded in favor of a more individualistic, liberal vision of citizenship, then a republic could begin to fail to produce citizens with the beliefs and behaviors necessary for the republic's preservation. During the American Founding, liberalism was embraced in conjunction with republicanism, and there was often a healthy balance between the republican emphasis on civic virtue and the liberal emphasis on individual rights. In recent decades, however, liberalism has become more narrowly defined by libertarians, who tend to deny claims that individuals have obligations to the community, to mean that individual liberty should never be restricted to advance the common good. The libertarian liberalism that has become more dominant identifies individual self-interest and personal choice as the most important aspects of our civic identity.

The degree to which individualism is prioritized within civic education will determine whether the vision of citizenship being promoted in American classrooms inspires students to transcend their own self-interest in the name of the general welfare or teaches them to reject concerns about collective well-being as "socialism" or "tyranny." Evidence that individualism is a powerful idea that can easily override concerns for the public good can be seen in behavior during the COVID-19 pandemic. The government appealed to people's sense of civic duty and concern for the community when promoting the wearing of face masks to minimize the spread of the virus. Many Americans willingly followed the government's requests and recommendations, but many resisted doing so on the grounds that they should not have to inconvenience themselves or limit their own personal freedom to protect other people. The division over whether people should be required to wear face masks eventually made its way to the public school system and created a hostile and anxious environment for educators and students alike.

The pandemic was a national crisis when the obligations of civic duty were strong, but many people were proudly defiant in not complying with public health recommendations. I do not blame civic education for our national failure to prioritize collective health. I also do not believe that the goal of civic education is to produce citizens who are unable to think for themselves or unwilling to challenge government requests, but the pandemic was a telling example of how deficient our vision of citizenship has become in recent decades. The United States prides itself on the level of patriotism displayed by its citizens, and Americans fondly recall historical examples when the public came together to overcome economic crises like the Great Depression and national security threats like World War II, but the American people arguably failed in the face of a public health crisis due to an excess of individualism. Civic education was not the cause of this failure, but the failure highlights the important role of civic education in a republic where the people are engaged in individual and collective self-government. Obviously, the protection of individual rights and promotion of individual freedom are central to the American political system, but the commitment to individualism must also be balanced at times with a commitment to equality and the general welfare. Civic education in American public schools has a role to play in cultivating a commitment to the ideals of republican self-government, which encompass more than simply a celebration of liberal individualism.

Political Theory to the Rescue?

What insights can political theory provide when asking questions about the content and aim of civic education in American public schools? While it may not be obvious that political theory has much to offer, it has long been the case that "political science has had a special relationship with civic education."[9] According to James Ceaser, a scholar of American political thought, "the connection between them flows almost directly from Aristotle's definition of political science" in which "political science was . . . invited to consider the proper kind of education for each regime type, a task that involved designing the ends or objectives of an educational program."[10] It follows that civic education would be especially important in republican regimes to prepare the next generation to preserve the ideals and practices of republican self-government. The United States was founded as a constitutional republic based on the political principles of liberalism, which renders Aristotle's observation that the content of civic education should match the type of regime somewhat problematic. While the American Founders were certainly inspired by the ideals of republicanism, the institutional design of the U.S. Constitution is more properly understood as being liberal in that it takes as its point of departure the assumption that republican civic virtue, while desirable and worth promoting, cannot be relied upon to avoid tyranny.

While both republicanism and liberalism inspired the American Founding, the machinery of the American political system, designed to protect individual liberty and avoid tyranny, takes its inspiration from liberalism. For example, the U.S. Constitution is designed to protect individual liberties from government interference. Yet the American Founders wanted American citizens to bring republican values to their interactions with the liberal machinery of government. According to Ceaser, a civic education that promotes republican values emphasizes "the inculcation of civic virtue, meaning that individual's devotion to the public good over his private good. This goal requires reaching every part of the individual's character and intellect. Civic education is all-consuming."[11] To define civic virtue, to identify which traits of character and intellectual skills characterize republican citizenship, and to articulate an acceptable rationale for public schools to provide such a normative civic education are not simple tasks theoretically or practically.

Ceaser, it should be noted, does not endorse a normative civic education that would promote a republican vision of citizenship. As he sees it, the notion that an excess of individualism should be remedied by a concerted effort to promote civic virtue is an inappropriate use of public schools and no longer qualifies as civic education. In his essay "The Role of Political Science and Political Scientists in Civic Education," he makes a distinction between civic education and political education. He uses the term political education to refer "to an educational program designed to undermine the existing regime and change it; its aim is transformation. Civic education is a program of education designed to preserve the existing regime; its aim is transmission."[12] While I find the distinction interesting, I doubt that it is practical to expect a democratic republic to simply transmit existing values when the political process itself is designed to allow for the evolution of values within society and law. Ceaser accuses progressives of capturing civic education and using it to promote change and reform, but preparation for participation in a republic necessarily involves teaching students how they can use the political system to effect change. The distinction between political and civic education seems odd and problematic, given that, for example, the definitions of freedom and equality have been expanded over time in American history to encompass equal rights and opportunity for more and more people only *after* popular reform movements organized to achieve change. In other words, whatever the status quo values are at any given moment, they are the result of changes in the past. It doesn't make much sense for civic education to *transmit* the values that are a result of historical change without also acknowledging and promoting the process of *transformation* that produced them.

To offer a response to the accusation that civic education is often co-opted inappropriately by those seeking to reform society, it seems that the theoretical confusion about the proper aims of civic education stems from the fact that the American Founders inhabited a historical moment when liberalism and republicanism overlapped philosophically and were drawn from simultaneously without much thought given to possible tensions that exist between them. Over time, liberalism and republicanism developed into distinct traditions, and political theorists increasingly highlighted their different theoretical implications. The legacy of the American Founding for American politics and civic education is captured in the summary that it "ostensibly fought to secure autonomy for virtuous citizens, [and] unleashed a passion for individual rights that eventually threatened to trample the virtue it was intended to facilitate."[13] Given that the ideals of republican civic virtue helped inspire the American Founding, but that the principles of liberal individualism have come to dominate American politics, the dilemma posed for civic education is quite complicated. Should civic education in the United States reflect, to the extent that they are distinct, the ideas of republicanism or liberalism? As it has developed historically in the United States, liberalism often prioritizes individual rights and personal freedom over notions of civic virtue and the common good. More importantly, for our discussion of civic education, political theorists often see liberalism as necessarily committed to neutrality on questions about how people should live. For example, some political theorists argue that a liberal democracy cannot endorse a "vision of the good life," because doing so would violate the personal autonomy at the heart of liberalism. The distinction Ceaser makes between political and civic education, and the degree to which liberalism or republicanism should inspire the content and aims of civic education, take on practical importance when considered in relation to some political theorists' concerns about government "neutrality" within a liberal democracy.[14] Yes, our liberal democracy is neutral in not telling people how to live or what to value (in general), but does that necessarily mean that our public schools must be neutral by not promoting a normative civic education? My central argument, in the context of the rise of an authoritarian ideology like Christian Nationalism, is that a liberal democracy, a constitutional republic, cannot afford to remain neutral on democracy as a way of life.

While some political theorists may lament, and criticize, liberal democracy's "neutrality," other theorists insist that such neutrality is never possible. Continuing to think in terms of the distinction between using civic education to transmit values or using political education to transform values, does civic education today, which often promotes liberal individualism while claiming to be neutral, already do what Ceaser claims it should not? A contemporary critic of liberalism, Patrick Deneen, insists that "liberalism has always been animated by a vision of how humans ought to live, but it masked these normative commitments in the guise of neutrality."[15] In other words, civic education is always teaching *something*. If it is prioritizing individualism over civic virtue or refusing to teach specific values to remain neutral, then it is already actively taking sides and endorsing a vision of citizenship. The next question, then, is to ask whether the civic education being taught in American public schools is providing a vision of citizenship that will preserve American democracy. If the answer is no, and if anti-democratic threats exist to the republic, then it is in the American people's collective self-interest to identify a vision of citizenship that will equip America's youth to defend American democracy. Doing so, however, will necessarily involve taking sides on normative questions and endorsing a "vision of good citizenship."

Given the degree to which Christian Nationalists are providing, to use Ceaser's term, an "all-consuming" civic education, whether through home schooling or private Christian schools, it seems imperative that the public school system respond with a normative civic education of its own. If one faction in society is normalizing anti-democratic beliefs and authoritarian behaviors, then the rest of society should not hesitate to defend and promote the beliefs and behaviors of liberal democracy. More to the point, now that Christian Nationalists are attempting to use public schools to promote their worldview, public schools, with the help of the community, must respond with a robust defense of diversity and inclusivity and unapologetic promotion of democratic values. Other critics of liberalism described as being republican or communitarian have objected to liberalism because "where liberals might support public education in hopes of equipping students to become autonomous individuals, capable of choosing their own ends and pursuing them effectively, communitarians might support public education in hopes of equipping students to become good citizens."[16] Christian Nationalism offers a vision of citizenship that tells young people that it is their patriotic and Christian duty to restore Christianity to its rightful place at the center of American society and politics. But what, according to critics of liberalism, does it mean to be a good citizen? What alternative to the Christian Nationalist vision can be constructed and promoted?

Liberal Democracy Requires Republican Civic Virtue

One of the distinctions between liberalism and republicanism that is most relevant to civic education, and useful for thinking about the COVID-19 pandemic, is the different conceptions of liberty that arise from each tradition. Political theorists such as Isaiah Berlin distinguish between positive and negative freedom when discussing individual liberty.[17] For example, negative freedom is understood as the absence of restraint or formal barriers. An individual enjoys negative freedom when they experience non-interference from the government or other people. Positive freedom is understood as the ability to realize one's potential and act in accordance with one's convictions. An individual enjoys positive freedom when they possess the resources to do what they want or willingly choose to act in accordance with an ideal they believe in. The example I often use when introducing these concepts to students is higher education. All students enjoy negative freedom when it comes to attending college, because there are no legal barriers such as racial or gender discrimination preventing them from attending the local community college. In this sense, they are "free" to go to college and so is everyone else. My students quickly develop puzzled expressions because they immediately identify reasons why this "freedom" is not quite real. For example, college costs money, and if an individual lacks the financial resources to pay for it, then their "freedom" to attend isn't very meaningful. Students only enjoy positive freedom when they have access to the resources necessary to use their freedom and act on their desire to attend.

It is at this moment that students begin to perceive the tension that can exist between liberty and equality, between individualism and the common good. Americans care deeply about both ideals, but often choose to prioritize liberty over equality. Republicanism, again, promotes active participation in politics and the exercise of civic virtue to pursue the common good. Republicanism, therefore, often implies egalitarianism because individuals must have an equal opportunity to participate in politics, and the pursuit of the common good tends to identify disparities that lead to calls for redistribution of resources. Americans care deeply about liberty and equality because both liberalism and republicanism inspired the American Founding. The adherents of liberalism, who tend to focus on individual freedom and protecting it from government interference, are often content if individuals possess negative freedom. To go one step further and ask what is necessary for individuals to truly have freedom in the positive sense often requires infringing on people's liberty elsewhere. For example, many Americans take it for granted that the K-12 public school system does not charge tuition. Everyone, regardless of whether they are attending school or have children doing so, is taxed to pay for the public school system. In this situation, Americans have chosen to prioritize the general welfare of society and common good over the rights of the individual to use their money how they want. The government infringes on everyone's economic freedom, through taxation, to provide equal access to educational opportunity that enables everyone to realize their potential. Furthermore, this is done not simply to produce an educated citizenry but also to empower each individual to live a meaningful life.

Michael Sandel, a critic of liberalism, argues in *Democracy's Discontent* that liberalism today promotes a negative version of liberty, which he sees as a deficient conception of freedom to underpin society, and by extension civic education, because such a conception does not promote active citizenship. Negative freedom, conceived of as non-interference, does not ennoble the individual to transcend their self-interest for the common good or communicate civic obligations that promote the general welfare. Liberalism, according to critics like Sandel, tends to minimize the ability of the government to interfere with the individual's freedom of choice about how to live. Prioritizing non-interference in this way in the context of civic education dilutes the promotion of civic obligations and civic virtue. Sandel draws on positive conceptions of freedom stemming from Aristotle, which "held that the purpose of politics was to cultivate the virtue, or moral excellence of citizens," to critique the fact that liberalism "does not see political life as concerned with the highest human ends or with the moral excellence of its citizens."[18] Sandel wants the liberal state to promote political participation and for citizens to identify with liberal democracy in a deep way. The aim is for individuals to feel a sense of civic duty and obligation to the community, and Sandel argues that "the republican tradition . . . may offer a corrective to our impoverished civic life."[19]

Maurizio Viroli, another critic of liberalism who shares some of Sandel's concerns about the excessive individualism that now characterizes liberal democracy, argues in *Republicanism* that "liberal liberty aims to protect individuals only from interferences, from actions interfering with their freedom of choice."[20] Viroli sees liberalism as prioritizing the individual's freedom over the general welfare of society. It follows that a civic education in a liberal democracy may communicate to young people that they have rights but not necessarily duties. Like Sandel, Viroli believes that republicanism has a role to play as "a theory not only of political liberty but also of the passions that political liberty needs" and insists that "liberty can survive only if citizens possess that special passion called civic virtue."[21] Both of them lament liberal democracy's failure to insist that individuals approach the role of citizen with specific values and dispositions, or even take the role of citizen seriously at all. At the heart of their criticism of liberalism is a desire to reinvigorate more active and virtuous approaches to citizenship. Sandel argues that "to share in self-rule ... requires that citizens possess, or come to acquire, certain qualities of character, or civic virtues" and that producing citizens with the needed virtues "requires a formative politics" and civic education that is not neutral on what constitutes good citizenship in a republic.[22]

Sandel sees republicanism as an alternative to liberalism because it "interprets rights in the light of a particular conception of the good society—the self-governing republic."[23] The significance for civic education is that rights would be taught in conjunction with the duties and obligations of civic life. Any attempt to increase political participation or cultivate a devotion to the general welfare will fail if the underlying conception of freedom is non-interference, which Sandel sees, perhaps unfairly, as fundamental to liberalism itself. In contrast, a "republican politics regards moral character as a public, not merely private, concern. In this sense, it attends to the identity, not just the interests, of its citizens."[24] If civic education were to shape identity by promoting civic virtue, then it would take on the "all-consuming" nature of the republican civic education that Ceaser rejected as political education.

What do these theoretical conversations between academics about different conceptions of freedom have to do with public education in America? They help us diagnose what is ailing American society so that we can identify possible remedies. The practical insight provided by academic "critics of liberalism" like Sandel and Viroli is that liberal democracy has become too focused on the individual and a particular definition of freedom that results in a lack of both civic participation and civic virtue. If the United States wants to preserve its constitutional republic, then the "neutral" liberal state must promote a normative "vision of good citizenship" that produces individuals committed, in their beliefs and behaviors, to liberal democracy.

Freedom, Civic Duty, and Public Health

The discussions taking place within political theory about freedom and republicanism are not just relevant to the task of identifying the type of civic education that will preserve American democracy. Political theory is also helpful in understanding recent challenges facing American public schools and considering the type of civic education that would encourage individuals to be concerned about the general welfare of society in addition to their individual freedom. For example, the requirement, or even just recommendation, to wear face masks during the COVID-19 pandemic became an extremely controversial political issue, at least in Texas, as individuals increasingly perceived the public health protocols as an infringement of their personal liberty. Many parents, including myself, were nervous to send their children to public schools early in the pandemic, because there was not a lot of data on how likely it was that the virus would spread within schools and then be brought home to vulnerable infants or elderly family members. We now know that public schools were often safer for children than society at large, because everyone inside schools, all students and staff, were required by law to follow strict protocols to wear masks and wash hands. Then, just as people's confidence about the safety of public schools was increasing, elected officials in states like Texas, with political and ideological motivations, no longer required masks to be worn and even passed laws forbidding school districts from continuing to require them. Once again, parents and educators were faced with uncertainty and anxiety about how safe public schools would be regarding the spread of COVID-19.

The wearing of face masks to reduce the spread of the virus was always a case study in people's civic and ethical commitments. Did people wear them out of self-interest simply to protect their own health? Did people also wear them because they understood that doing so reduced other people's risk? Once younger and healthier people realized that their personal risk was low, would they continue to wear them to protect older and more vulnerable people? One of the most important reasons to wear face masks to minimize the spread of the virus, which was consistently but for some reason not effectively communicated, was to reduce the number of people in local hospitals with severe cases of the virus. The reason is that hospitals could become overwhelmed with patients and unable to help people with other health complications. So, again, there were individual and collective rationales for wearing a face mask, but many individuals refused to do so, especially in states like Texas, as a point of pride.

Why did people refuse to wear face masks during the height of the pandemic? Political theory would suggest that many people understand freedom in the libertarian liberal sense, as negative freedom, where individuals are not interfered with by government. Why were so many people unwilling to wear face masks to help protect others or prevent hospitals from becoming overwhelmed? One explanation is that the current vision of citizenship lacks a healthy balance between the liberal commitment to individual freedom or personal choice and the republican emphasis on the common good and recognition of civic obligations to the community. In Texas public schools, this case study played out differently in each school district, because, unlike in many smaller states, the state government does not control local education policy. Instead, local policy is decided by over 1,000 independent school districts in rural, suburban, or urban areas.

When Governor Greg Abbott, a Republican, issued Executive Order GA-38 that forbid any school district from requiring face masks, school districts in Houston responded in a variety of ways. Some courageously defied the governor and attempted to mandate masks anyway. Others encouraged students and staff to voluntarily wear face masks to prevent unnecessary spread of the virus. These districts, without necessarily realizing it, were appealing to the republican ideal of civic virtue. While the governor had prevented the school districts from *requiring* face masks, the most effective way to minimize spread, there was nothing to prevent students and staff from *voluntarily* doing what was in the best interest of their community. If district leadership, like the school board trustees and superintendent, appealed to people's civic obligations to prioritize the collective well-being of the community, even if it required personal inconvenience, then people might choose to answer the civic call.

Individuals who viewed mask mandates through the lens of negative freedom only saw themselves as free when they were not being told what to do by the government, when they enjoyed non-interference. However, the freedom of being at school all day without a face mask is also the "freedom" to get the coronavirus or spread it to family and friends. Those who remained vulnerable to the virus, which included *all* students since vaccines were not yet available for them, were not free at all. Yes, students could choose to wear a face mask voluntarily, and many did, but they were forced to spend hours in close proximity to people who were not wearing face masks and who did not necessarily take the virus seriously.

The freedom enjoyed by those who did not want to wear masks was experienced as the opposite of freedom, almost as an imprisonment, by those who felt vulnerable being forced to share public space with people who disregarded public health recommendations. In this situation, one group's negative freedom came at the expense of another group's positive freedom to the detriment of the entire community. In the opposite situation where everyone is required to wear face masks, the freedom of one group is infringed on to the benefit of the entire community because everyone is safe. The republican ideal of civic virtue would ask that individuals willingly choose to limit their freedom by voluntarily wearing a face mask that creates freedom for everyone to inhabit public space safely during a pandemic.

I view the promotion of a normative civic education in a similar way. The liberal state cannot coerce individuals to possess civic virtue, mandate that they vote, or require them to care about the common good, but American public schools can offer students a normative "vision of good citizenship" that proudly declares participation in democratic self-government a desirable and meaningful way to live. Students can choose to embrace a normative civic education or not. The point is that public schools should not feel the need to remain neutral about the benefits of a democratic way of life. Some school districts chose not to remain neutral about the public health benefits of wearing face masks during a pandemic. They encouraged their students and staff to be the best versions of themselves by recognizing both individual and collective reasons to embrace their civic duty. They appealed to the republican ideal of civic virtue and a more positive conception of freedom wherein individuals chose to do what was right for the community, which in turn was beneficial for themselves. Unfortunately, a nearby school district, where my wife happened to teach at the time, did no such thing.

A Case of Partisan Neutrality

Unlike most suburban districts in Houston, one school district refused to encourage students or staff to wear masks or even publicly acknowledge the public health benefits of wearing them. The school district's mask policy, as stated in their "Back-to-School Health & Safety Plan," stated: "Per Executive Order GA-38, no employee, student, or visitor is required to wear a mask or face covering, but all employees, students, and visitors are allowed to wear a mask or face covering if they choose to do so." When I first read the policy, I was shocked that there was no language encouraging mask wearing, summarizing the rationale for wearing masks voluntarily, or stating the public health benefits of doing so. The language about being "allowed" to wear a mask made it seem like it was unnecessary. It made it seem like the people who believed in the benefits of wearing face masks were being appeased. It reminded me of negative freedom, the idea of non-interference, and of the tendency within a liberal society to focus on personal choice.

Perhaps they thought that they were remaining neutral on the issue, but they were embracing a particular conception of freedom and vision of citizenship. Whether consciously or not, they were taking sides and they were aligning themselves with radical individualism. While individuals had many reasons for disliking face masks or declining to wear them, it seemed that a large percentage who chose not to wear them were consciously aware of a political or ideological motivation to resist what they saw as government oppression or tyranny. They simply were not going to let the government tell them what to do, even if there was a public health rationale. People proudly defied or ignored public health recommendations in the name of individual liberty. The school district tacitly endorsed those who believed that individual freedom was more important than public health by refusing to ask their students and staff to think about the general welfare of their community.

If the district wanted to focus on personal choice, then they could have focused on those individuals who chose *not* to wear masks. The school district's policy could have emphasized the personal risk that individuals were taking if they chose not to wear masks. The expectation could have been that people should voluntarily wear face masks to protect themselves and the people around them, but that due to the governor's decision, individuals were allowed to *not* wear a mask if they chose. It was clear to me that the school district had unnecessarily limited itself to a false choice between mandating face masks or doing absolutely nothing to encourage them. This was in August 2021, so I decided to attend the next school board meeting before the new school year started.

While adults had been eligible for vaccines for six months, children still did not have access. Surely, I thought, public schools should be promoting face masks until children have access to a vaccine. I was determined to provide the school district what I believed was a common-sense path forward that would promote public health and respect the differences of opinion that existed on the topic. Getting vaccinated may be a personal choice, but the spread of the virus impacts the entire community. I was optimistic that a local government like a school board would choose to promote responsible behavior based on expert medical advice to minimize the spread of a deadly virus.

I made the following remarks:

> Lord knows we all wanted a more normal school year, but the unfortunate fact is that the Delta variant is here. It is a fact that our kids are more likely to get COVID this fall than last fall because the Delta variant is far more transmissible. It is a fact that more children are in the ICU in Houston right now than at any point during the pandemic. COVID is not over. For our kids, COVID is worse now than ever.
>
> The Governor's misguided executive order does not prevent [the district] from creating and promoting a culture of mask wearing. The CDC, the American Academy of Pediatrics, and Texas Children's Hospital all recommend universal mask wearing by students and staff. Opposition to mask wearing is political. Support for mask wearing is based on empirical evidence that it stops the spread of COVID. To not openly promote masks because some have a political objection to them is to allow politics to interfere with sound medical advice.
>
> I urge you to put the safety of students ahead of politics and immediately revise the language in the district's "Health & Safety Plan" regarding masks, which reads: "individuals are allowed to wear a mask if they choose to do so." This language is insufficient, and I urge you to "strongly recommend and encourage" that all students and staff wear masks. Please lead by example and set expectations for [the district] that will promote health and safety this school year. If a campus culture can discourage drug use or bullying, then surely it can discourage the unnecessary spread of a deadly virus.

After explaining to the school board and superintendent that the district had a practical and measured way to promote health and safety without wading into the politics of mask mandates, I felt proud that I had used my voice to protect students, teachers, and the entire community. None of what I said seemed controversial to me. In fact, it seemed obvious. As school districts across Texas decided to either defy Governor Abbott or encourage people to voluntarily wear face masks, this school district remained silent. Then, Harris County challenged the legality of Governor Abbott's executive order by requiring all school districts within the county to once again mandate face masks. The district's response was relevant to our discussion of citizenship and civic education. The district stated, "As a school district committed to teaching and modeling civic responsibility for our students, [we] will continue to follow the law." To be clear, the law the district insisted it would follow was the governor's controversial executive order, not Harris County's.

As a civic educator, I was appalled that a school district would describe partisan allegiance using the words "civic responsibility." Unlike neighboring suburban districts in Houston, the district was demonstrating zero civic responsibility with their face mask policy. If they wanted to showcase civic responsibility, then they could have encouraged individuals to act for the good of the *community* by voluntarily doing what public health experts recommended. If the district truly wanted to model civic responsibility, then they could have done what neighboring districts did and encouraged students and staff to wear masks. I found it outrageous that a school district would use the words "civic responsibility" to characterize their decision to follow an executive order that undermined *public* health and prevented *civic* leaders from protecting the *community*.

At the time, I faulted the district for remaining neutral when they needed to take a stand. Now, I see the actions of the school board and superintendent in a different light. They weren't just remaining neutral, but they were also actively or tacitly doing the bidding of Christian Nationalists who were opposed to face masks. Why was district leadership so unwilling to simply state that wearing face masks was an effective way to minimize the spread of the virus? It is an objective, scientific, medical fact that wearing face masks is an effective way to prevent the spread of COVID-19 within schools absent the availability of vaccines. So, how can it be controversial to simply share with the community what public health experts know and recommend? As Perry and Gorski argue in *The Flag and the Cross*, Christian Nationalists understand freedom in a specifically "libertarian way, as freedom from restrictions, especially by the government."[25]

It was an election year, and multiple school board trustees were running for reelection. Were they afraid that if they encouraged students and staff to wear face masks, they would lose support from Christian Nationalist voters? It is impossible to know what their motivations were, but it is alarming to think that a minority faction could so scare local leaders that they would disregard expert medical advice. If trustees were too scared of anti-mask Christian Nationalist voters to actively promote public health, then they willingly put their own political self-interest ahead of the safety of 54,000 students and staff. Alternatively, the trustees may have been anti-mask Christian Nationalists themselves. In either case, this school district provides a cautionary tale. If local, state, and national leaders are too scared to stand up to Christian Nationalists, then liberal democracy and our democratic way of life will succumb to authoritarian threats. If voters don't mobilize to defend liberal democracy from Christian Nationalism, then local, state, and national institutions can become captured by an authoritarian faction that makes decisions in accordance with their own Christian Nationalist worldview. The American republic needs political leaders at all levels of government to act with courage, not cowardice; and American public schools need a "vision of good citizenship" that inspires the next generation to do the same.

Takeaways for Elected Officials and School Administrators

- Understand that when remaining "neutral," you may be taking sides.
- When making decisions, you must think about the ideological assumptions or partisan ramifications of your actions.
- Everyone is a leader with power and responsibility: from the state capitol to the school board to the campus.
- Policymakers, from state legislators to school board trustees, must publicly reject Christian Nationalist policies and uphold the principles of liberal democracy.
- Denouncing Christian Nationalism is not sufficient; the principles of liberal democracy must be celebrated and promoted.
- Elected officials and school administrators must act as "Ambassadors" of liberal democracy to counteract the proponents of Christian Nationalism.

Notes

1 "Brutus I," in *The Anti-Federalist Writings of the Melancton Smith Circle*, eds. Michael Zuckert and Derek Webb (Indianapolis: Liberty Fund, 2009), 174.
2 James Madison, "Federalist 10," in *The Federalist* (New York: Barnes and Noble Classics, 2006), 55.
3 Ibid., 56.
4 Ibid.
5 Glenn Thrush, "We're Not a Democracy, Says Mike Lee, a Republican Senator. That's a Good Thing, He Adds," *New York Times*, October 8, 2020.
6 Madison, "Federalist 10," 55.
7 Terence Ball and Richard Dagger, *Political Ideologies and the Democratic Ideal* (New York: Pearson, 2004), 25.
8 "Declaration of Independence."
9 James Ceaser, *The Role of Political Science and Political Scientists in Civic Education* (American Enterprise Institute, 2013), 2, https://www.aei.org/wp-content/uploads/2013/08/-the-role-of-political-science-and-political-scientists-in-civic-education_102917311507.pdf.

10 Ibid.
11 Ibid., 3.
12 Ibid., 10.
13 James Kloppenberg, *The Virtues of Liberalism* (New York: Oxford University Press, 1998), 168.
14 Michael Sandel, *Democracy's Discontent* (Cambridge: Harvard University Press, 1996).
15 Patrick Deneen, *Why Liberalism Failed* (New Haven: Yale University Press, 2018), 188.
16 Michael Sandel, "Introduction," in *Liberalism and Its Critics*, ed. Sandel (New York University Press, 1984), 6.
17 Isaiah Berlin, "Two Concepts of Liberty," in *Liberalism and Its Critics*, 16.
18 Sandel, *Democracy's Discontent*, 7.
19 Ibid., 6.
20 Maurizio Viroli, *Republicanism* (New York: Hill and Wang, 2002), 12.
21 Ibid., 12.
22 Sandel, *Democracy's Discontent*, 6.
23 Ibid., 25.
24 Ibid.
25 Philip S. Gorski and Samuel L. Perry, *The Flag and the Cross: White Christian Nationalism and the Threat to American Democracy* (New York: Oxford University Press, 2022), 7.

3 Moving From Neutral to Normative

Imagining a Normative Civic Education

Thus far, I have made the claim that the civic mission of American public schools is currently threatened by Christian Nationalism, an authoritarian and antidemocratic worldview. Given that context, I have argued that it is imperative for American public schools to endorse a normative civic education that promotes a "vision of good citizenship" to preserve liberal democracy. The argument that a particular civic education is necessary to achieve a specific goal is an instrumental justification that regards civic education as a means to an end. While there is certainly a strong instrumental justification for a normative civic education that will help preserve the American republic, it may also be the case that a normative civic education has intrinsic worth by promoting a democratic way of life. We will return to the different rationales that exist for embracing a normative civic education in a later chapter, but first we must consider what a normative civic education would look like and evaluate whether civic education is already normative in certain respects. An examination of what civic education already does to preserve liberal democracy and what it could do to further promote a democratic way of life highlights why Christian Nationalists are proactively trying to undermine and hijack the civic mission of American public schools.

Political theorists have written extensively about public education in a liberal democracy. Liberals such as William Galston and Amy Gutmann have emphasized the importance of respecting diversity and encouraging rational deliberation, while republicans such as Richard Dagger and Thomas Spragens have focused on cultivating civic virtue and promoting active participation in politics. Dagger, a republican "critic of liberalism," promotes autonomy and civic virtue as intrinsically valuable for the individual but does not go so far as to claim that the individual must possess these traits to live a "good life." In *Civic Virtues*, he argues that a revival of republican civic virtue is desirable but insists that

> a republican liberal will be too much of a liberal to believe that politics is either the only or the highest good in life, but ... enough of a republican to insist that the public business requires some attention and effort on the part of the citizen.[1]

DOI: 10.4324/9781032686059-3

Dagger, like Sandel, wants to promote political participation, and he believes that autonomy and civic virtue must be cultivated as necessary components of active citizenship. Yet, unlike Sandel, who promotes political participation itself as a "vision of the good life," Dagger promotes autonomy as something with intrinsic worth that happens to make political participation and self-government possible. In other words, a normative "vision good of citizenship" using Dagger's approach would not be forced on people by the government, but it would be encouraged as a natural utilization of the autonomy that is already cultivated through public education. We must ask, though, can public schools claim to be "neutral" if they promote autonomy and civic virtue as Dagger recommends?

William Galston, a liberal, is skeptical that a liberal democracy can be truly neutral. He insists that "no form of political life can be justified without some view of what is good for individuals. In practice, liberal theorists covertly employ theories of the good."[2] Galston argues in *Liberal Purposes* that "liberalism cannot . . . be understood as broadly neutral concerning the human good"[3] and that "the liberal state must become far more aware of, and far more actively involved in reproducing, the conditions necessary to its own health and perpetuation."[4] Galston shares Sandel's concern about the ability of liberal democracy to preserve itself, and he identifies a set of "liberal virtues" that he considers valuable instrumentally as a "means to the preservation of liberal societies and institutions."[5] However, unlike Dagger's promotion of autonomy, Galston does not consider his "liberal virtues" intrinsically valuable traits necessary for human flourishing. Some of his examples of "liberal virtues" include courage, law-abidingness, loyalty, and moderation.

While Galston acknowledges that a liberal democracy must consciously produce citizens with "liberal virtues," he insists that "the liberal citizen is not the same as the civic republican citizen . . . there is no duty to participate actively in politics, no requirement to . . . subordinate personal interest to the common good."[6] He believes that public schools must intentionally develop "liberal virtues," but he is concerned about respect for religious diversity, explicitly rejects the idea that rational autonomy is a necessary ingredient of citizenship in a liberal democracy, and criticizes the notion that civic education should promote it. In the present historical context, Galston's defense of diversity can be weaponized by Christian Nationalists to criticize critical thinking, argumentation based on verifiable fact, and other skills necessary to democratic self-government. If a faction of Christian Nationalists can insist that preparation for citizenship is incompatible with their political or religious worldview, then the civic mission of public schools can be co-opted by anti-democratic and authoritarian movements.

Amy Gutmann claims in *Democratic Education* that liberal theorists who want to promote individual autonomy through civic education fail to appreciate the disagreements that exist over what conception of freedom is correct and should be promoted in public schools. She proposes a "democratic" theory of education that promotes the capacity of rational deliberation as the aim of civic education. She recognizes that promoting rational deliberation is an endorsement of a way of life and says that "our task therefore is to find a more inclusive ground for justifying non-neutrality in education."[7] Gutmann insists that due to the deep disagreements that persist about the "good life," the government cannot start with an end and provide a civic education designed to achieve that end; all that is permitted is to prepare individuals "to deliberate among alternative ways of personal and political life."[8] This position is no longer tenable regarding civic education after the January 6th Insurrection and the rise of Christian Nationalism. American public schools must start with an end, the preservation of liberal democracy and promotion of a democratic way of life, then provide a civic education that cultivates the beliefs and behaviors that will preserve that way of life.

In her promotion of rational deliberation as the aim of civic education, Gutmann seems to disregard how central individual autonomy and civic virtue are to the activity of deliberation itself. Galston, writing after Gutmann, takes issue with the preoccupation of cultivating rational deliberation absent any "liberal virtues" to guide and motivate the activity. He also worries that diversity may suffer in the face of rational deliberation that lacks "liberal virtues" such as tolerance. In the end, public schools in a liberal democracy cannot remain neutral on democracy, and the rational deliberation that takes place within a self-governing society requires rational autonomy and civic virtue to protect liberal democracy from illiberal or authoritarian factions. Both Galston and Gutmann understand that a liberal democracy is not and cannot be neutral regarding civic education, but they diverge on what type of civic education a liberal society needs to remain liberal. Galston insists that a liberal society should protect diversity instead of cultivating rational autonomy. Gutmann seemingly agrees with Galston's rejection of rational autonomy as the aim of civic education, but then she promotes a form of rational deliberation that Galston argues will leave diversity vulnerable to attack. Both theorists attempt to provide a more normative task for civic education, but they fail to satisfactorily identify what a normative civic education in a liberal democracy should promote to preserve liberal democracy itself.

Rational Autonomy and Civic Virtue

Somewhat similar to Richard Dagger's synthesis between liberalism and republicanism that seeks to combine a renewal of civic virtue with respect for individual autonomy, Thomas Spragens offers "a normative conception of liberal democracy" called "civic liberalism." He claims in *Civic Liberalism* that "the key question . . . is whether the liberal commitment to individual freedoms and the civic republican pursuit of community and civic virtue are merely in tension or are genuinely irreconcilable."[9] His proposal for "civic liberalism" attempts to refocus the liberal tradition and its promotion of liberty by arguing that "the liberty treasured by that tradition is best understood as the achievement of autonomy."[10] In addition to the promotion of autonomy, Spragens, like Galston, develops a list of "liberal civic virtues" that characterize liberal citizenship in a republic. He disagrees with Galston that rational autonomy is not a necessary component of citizenship in a liberal democracy, but he does not justify the promotion of rational autonomy or civic virtue by insisting that they have intrinsic value as part of the "good life." Spragens claims that rational autonomy should be understood as liberal liberty, and as such, something to be developed through civic education in public schools, but not endorsed as a "vision of the good life" or necessary for human flourishing.

Galston objects to rational autonomy as the goal of civic education because it constitutes a distinct way of life that may undermine the diversity of ways of life within a liberal society; in particular, deeply religious ways of living. He argues in "Two Concepts of Liberalism" that "the personal liberty the state must defend is the liberty not to be coerced into, or trapped within, ways of life."[11] He considers the promotion of rational autonomy as a step beyond the appropriate limits of power in a liberal society because he interprets autonomy as synonymous with individual choice, which he does not consider essential to the preservation of liberal society. Galston insists that "to place an ideal of autonomous choice . . . at the core of liberalism is in fact to narrow the range of possibilities within liberal societies" and that "rather than taking autonomy or critical reflection as our point of departure, what we need instead is an account of liberalism that gives diversity its due."[12] In the context of civic education, a respect for diversity that permits Christian Nationalists to attack LGBTQ+ inclusion on the grounds that it violates religious liberty undermines the civic mission of public schools and permits anti-democratic ways of life to undermine the pluralism of a democratic society. In other words, it makes no sense to limit the promotion of rational autonomy in public schools on the grounds that it offends groups that are opposed to ways of life that empower individuals to actively choose their religious commitments rather than passively inherit them. It is one thing to respect religious separatists who desire to be left alone by the government, but it is something else entirely to respect Christian Nationalist attempts to use public schools to promote a worldview at odds with individual autonomy, diversity, and pluralism.

Gutmann argues that "a democratic state must aid children in developing the capacity to understand and to evaluate competing conceptions of the good life and good society"[13] and that the government's power to educate is only limited by the principle of "non-repression," which would prevent it from "using education to restrict rational deliberation of competing conceptions of the good life and the good society."[14] Gutmann, it seems, believes that democratic deliberation requires the ability to critically examine a variety of views about how to live, including one's own views, but this type of self-reflection is precisely what Galston regards as the individual autonomy that the state should not impose on individuals. Gutmann clearly does value some form of rational autonomy, but she calls it "rational deliberation" and justifies its promotion through civic education on instrumental grounds as necessary for democratic self-government. Dagger offers a fuller version of individual autonomy that sees it as a fundamental right to be exercised in varying degrees. He argues that "autonomy is the ability or capacity to govern oneself"[15] and "that every person is entitled to exercise his or her capacity to lead a self-governed life."[16] However, unlike the libertarian liberal claim that autonomy guarantees maximum individual freedom as non-interference, Dagger insists that autonomy should be understood as a human right "that every person shares with every other person, and this limits what we may do *as a matter of right*."[17] Such an understanding of autonomy points toward our shared civic obligations and collective welfare instead of our individual liberty.

Dagger offers a version of individual autonomy that is geared more toward the exercise of civic virtue and recognition of civic duties. In contrast to standard liberal conceptions of autonomy, Dagger insists:

> [P]eople are self-legislating, autonomous . . . to the extent that they *choose* the principles by which they live. But if they truly choose the principles that guide their conduct, autonomous people must *be aware* of the alternatives from which they can choose and *be able* to think critically about them.[18]

In other words, to return to the previous chapter's discussion of face masks, a normative civic education in a liberal democracy should promote the type of rational autonomy and civic virtue that could result in students choosing to wear face masks to benefit the community. The "vision of good citizenship" encouraged, but not coerced, by such a civic education would equip individuals to think for themselves about what is in their individual and collective self-interest and act accordingly. Likewise, the United States needs a normative civic education that will equip and encourage individuals to choose liberal democracy as a desirable form of government and way of life.

While it could be conceded that the promotion of rational autonomy is a "vision of the good life," Dagger points out that "republican liberalism seeks to *promote* and *cultivate*, but not to *maximize*, certain values."[19] Disagreements between political theorists over the role and importance of autonomy within civic education and democratic self-government can also be understood in reference to the different conceptions of freedom discussed in the previous chapter. According to Isaiah Berlin, "if freedom is understood as self-realization, the crucial element of noncoercion is in danger of being lost"[20] because some authority may impose on an individual a vision of what the individual should realize but does not endorse. For Berlin, the fact that individuals could be compelled to live a certain way or pursue a certain end constitutes the main danger of "positive" conceptions of liberty, which is why he promotes the "negative" conception of liberty as a safer bet for the protection of individual rights. Spragens claims that "Berlin's argument taken as a whole is analytically inadequate . . .

normatively misleading . . . [and] inappropriately dichotomous."[21] He locates the genesis of the divide between liberals and republicans at Berlin's characterization of autonomy as a form of "positive" liberty. Spragens defines autonomy as the opposite of dependency and insists that the aim of overcoming dependency is what united liberals, such as John Locke, and those inspired by republicanism, such as Thomas Jefferson. He insists that "the fundamental human good of autonomy . . . is the transcendence of this dependency . . . so that one has the capacity to be self-directing."[22] From the standpoint of Spragens' "civic liberalism," liberty as autonomy is neither "negative" nor "positive" and should be "understood as a constitutive good rather than an intrinsic or instrumental good."[23]

In the context of our discussion of normative civic education, one of the most significant questions is whether American public schools can promote a "vision of good citizenship" that some may interpret as indistinguishable from a "vision of the good life." For Spragens, it is because autonomy is conceived of as something to be cultivated and optimized that the government is justified in promoting it as one "vision of the good life," and this is similar to Dagger's insistence that "republican liberalism" can legitimately promote autonomy as long as it does not require maximizing it for its own sake. For both theorists, the value of individual autonomy, while significant for politics, is not dependent on politics for its worth. Spragens insists that autonomy is much more than an instrumental good and that "civic liberalism . . . tends to understand autonomy as an ethical good with import and application that exceed the political domain."[24] Again, a discussion about the rationale for embracing a normative civic education will come later, but there is a clear divide between theorists over whether individual autonomy has instrumental or intrinsic worth. Today, Christian Nationalists are attacking the notion that public schools should empower students to think for themselves about American history, gender and sexual identity, and scientific theories, especially if doing so results in students embracing views contrary to those of their parents. Christian Nationalists, characterizing their demands as the restoration of "parental rights," insist instead that schools not teach or promote anything that contradicts the views of parents. In this context, I argue, it is imperative that public schools promote individual autonomy as intrinsically valuable for students and instrumentally beneficial for American democracy.

Autonomy, a common concern of many liberal and republican theorists, is not the only important characteristic of a normative civic education. Civic virtue, particularly when defined as active participation in politics, is considered necessary by many political theorists to preserve liberal democracy. Dagger emphasizes civic virtue in conjunction with individual autonomy as an answer to the republican critique of liberalism's excessive individualism without insisting that political participation is necessary to achieve the "good life." He summarizes his republican liberal civic virtues as "respect[ing] individual rights, valu[ing] autonomy, tolerat[ing] different opinions and beliefs, play[ing] fair, cherish[ing] civic memory, and tak[ing] an active part in the life of the community."[25] As with Gutmann's promotion of rational deliberation and other democratic beliefs and behaviors, the civic virtue that Dagger promotes, while justified on instrumental grounds as being good for citizenship, is nonetheless also good for the individual in general. Autonomy, tolerance, and fair play are not simply instrumental goods that serve democracy well, they are intrinsic goods that serve individuals and society well. However, Dagger is hesitant to equate the beliefs and behaviors of "good citizenship" with those of the "good life." Crucial to our discussion of the content of a normative civic education, many political theorists share an unwillingness to concede that an endorsement of a "vision of good citizenship" may be barely distinguishable from a "vision of the good life."

Spragens identifies an even more comprehensive list of civic virtues than Galston and Dagger, but he argues that a liberal democracy should not be "in the business of telling its citizens how to be good, even when the virtues in question are political or civic and not comprehensive in their scope and rationale."[26] Spragens does not believe that civic education should be the main engine for producing civic virtue and that "the liberal virtues must be inculcated more by the institutions of civil society than by the state."[27] It is worth questioning whether civil society is equipped today to promote the liberal virtues conducive to active political participation and the preservation of the American republic. While an organization such as the Girl Scouts of America may empower young girls with values compatible with active citizenship and republican self-government, how many churches or private schools are promoting a Christian Nationalist worldview at odds with liberal democracy? In other words, it is not clear that civil society is prepared to do the important civic work that is needed at this moment in American history to preserve American democracy and a democratic way of life. Spragens does allow a role for American public schools in conceding that it is "acceptable for public institutions involved in the socialization of the young to thematize and seek to foster the liberal civic virtues under the rubric of good citizenship,"[28] but then also insists that "character education in public schools in a liberal society should not consist in catechizing students in the norms of good citizenship."[29] Again, given the reality of private Christian schools catechizing their students in the assumptions of Christian Nationalism wherein a civic duty to work to erode the separation of church and state and promote Christianity in the public sphere is cultivated, it is necessary for American public schools to protect American democracy by overtly promoting a democratic way of life.

Dagger insists that "for republican liberals, part of the point of education is to help people live autonomously"[30] and that "fostering autonomy and civic virtue ought to be, and can be, the acknowledged aims of public schools."[31] He laments that schools do not have a clear civic purpose and argues that "the obvious solution . . . is to find or forge a consensus on the proper purpose, or purposes, of education."[32] The rise of Christian Nationalism makes it clear that a consensus on the role of public education is nowhere on the horizon, and far from seeking to identify a purpose that all Americans can agree on, it is necessary for American public schools to protect American democracy from the threat of Christian Nationalism. While Dagger calls for public schools to take on a more normative role, his prescription for what a normative civic education should consist of is lacking in detail. On the other hand, Spragens provides the content of a robust civic education, but he denies that it is intrinsically beneficial or should be promoted by public schools.

Andrew Peterson, in *Civic Republicanism and Civic Education*, explores possible applications of the academic debates between political theorists to civic education itself. He writes that "the term civic education refers to any formative attempt to teach the knowledge, skills, or dispositions required for citizenship"[33] and that "civic republicanism embodies an active conception of what it means to be a citizen, with citizenship defined *as a practice*."[34] He aptly describes what could be the civic education envisioned by Gutmann and Galston by arguing that "a liberal informed civic education concerns itself primarily with an understanding of the rights of a citizen and the development of certain capacities, such as critical thinking, tolerance and respect, required to secure and protect such individual rights."[35] Peterson mainly discusses the application of republican ideas to civic education within the context of education policy in Great Britain, but he also analyzes civic education in Canada and the United States.

Peterson identifies four principles of a revived "civic republican" approach to civic education within liberal democracies: recognition of civic obligations, awareness of the common good, possession of civic virtue, and preparation for deliberation.[36] Whether political theorists or policymakers recognize it or not, the educational process is inherently engaged in promoting the development of specific skills, beliefs, behaviors, dispositions, and values. In other words, "there is little that is morally neutral about civic education—the attempt to train young people to be good citizens and to engage in civic life."[37] It is clear that civic education is already normative, and it only seems appropriate that "as a matter of accountability, [we] ought to explain—both to the youth [we] serve and to other adults—which civic values and habits [we] are trying to develop, and why."[38] In other words, in reference to Patrick Deneen's accusation that liberalism masks its "normative commitments," it is time for liberal democracy to take off the mask and own its values in the face of Christian Nationalist threats.

Diversity, Equity, and Inclusion, Oh My!

As our survey of the academic debates between liberal and republican theorists has demonstrated, some version of individual autonomy and concept of civic virtue are present in any discussion about what a normative civic education in a liberal democracy should include. It is also clear that public schools are already providing a normative civic education to some degree, whether in a positive manner by integrating some form of "character education" that promotes specific values or traits or in a negative manner by emphasizing individualism at the expense of civic virtue. In other words, some "vision of good citizenship" is already being promoted implicitly or explicitly. The question we must ask is whether the "vision of good citizenship" being promoted is right for the current historical moment where democratic values and American democracy itself are under attack from a minority faction of Christian Nationalists. American public schools are clearly teaching *some* values and behaviors; otherwise, Christian Nationalists wouldn't be accusing them of indoctrinating students with a "woke" agenda. That is not to say that there is any truth to the claim that a "woke" agenda exists within public schools; it simply proves that schools are teaching students *something* that Christian Nationalists find threatening to their worldview and agenda. So, what are students in public schools learning that Christian Nationalists find so triggering? Why do Christian Nationalists now insist on "safe spaces" for their children?

Over the last decade, the United States has experienced a rapid cultural shift in support of LGBTQ+ rights and equality. Recall that in 2005 Republicans were promoting a constitutional amendment to ban same-sex marriage nationwide. By 2015, same-sex marriage was not only supported by a large majority of the American public, but it was also legal nationwide.[39] The public's increasing tolerance, and celebration, of the LGBTQ+ community trickled down into the public school system not necessarily through formal programs or classroom instruction, but simply in the interactions that students had with peers and teachers who were members of the LGBTQ+ community. Students from highly conservative and religious families interacted with other students who were "out," and social acceptance of LGBTQ+ individuals became normalized for many. Even if their parents or pastor disapproved of same-sex marriage or generally believed that a "gay lifestyle" was sinful, they knew peers at school who made narratives about "depravity" almost impossible to agree with. You can be told that someone is a threat to you or society 1,000 times, but if that person sits next to you every day in Algebra II and you both like the same TikTok channels or Takis, then it is going to be hard to perpetuate homophobia. Gen Z, the youth of America, simply do not care about sexual orientation to the degree that their conservative parents want them to. Where their parents see an "LGBTQ+ agenda" in the public schools, they just see 21st-century America. Most importantly, they just see their friends.

Christian Nationalist parents are livid about the increase in tolerance toward the LGBTQ+ community and their inability to transmit their homophobia to their children. They are convinced that their children accept the LGBTQ+ community because the public schools taught them to do so and that's why they are demanding that programs like No Place for Hate be canceled and books depicting same-sex relationships be taken out of school libraries. Their anger comes out in school board meetings when they accuse administrators, teachers, or parents who disagree with banning books of being "groomers" who want to sexualize children and promote the "gay agenda." Their anger is evident when they oppose the inclusion of LGBTQ+ civil rights history in social studies classes. How dare teachers portray, Christian Nationalist parents protest, the advancement of equal rights for the LGBTQ+ community as progress analogous to other civil rights movements for gender and racial equality. They believe that such instruction is biased against religious beliefs because presenting LGBTQ+ equality in a positive light implies that opposition to LGBTQ+ equality rooted in religious objections is somehow discriminatory. Well, it *is* discriminatory. Just like opposition to gender and racial equality rooted in religious objections was discriminatory.

Having taught high school social studies for nine years, I am familiar with what happens in the classroom. For example, the teacher talks about some of the political and religious justifications that were used historically to oppose gender and racial equality; then, students start to connect the dots to today's political and religious objections to LGBTQ+ equality. The students then think for themselves and decide that not only is discrimination based on gender and race wrong, but discrimination based on sexual orientation is wrong too. They decide that their homophobic parents and pastor are simply the 21st-century version of the photos they see in their textbooks of angry White people screaming against the integration of schools and restaurants in the 1960s. Contrary to the accusations leveled at teachers, discussing the advancement of LGBTQ+ equality and rights in the context of other civil rights movements is not indoctrination, even if it has the effect of creating a learning environment that may feel hostile to those who claim that LGBTQ+ rights violate religious liberty.

When students decide for themselves that they support, or are simply indifferent to, LGBTQ+ equality, then parents feel that they have "lost the battle" and that public schools have interfered with their "parental rights" to transmit their religious beliefs to their children. They demand that schools stop teaching the history of LGBTQ+ civil rights, that teachers not be allowed to disclose their sexual orientation to students, that programs promoting tolerance and inclusion be stopped, that books depicting the personal exploration of sexual identity be banned, and that digital resources about the LGBTQ+ community be blocked online. In other words, if children learn history, interact with other humans, or read a book, then they might think for themselves and decide that they think differently from their parents. An educational experience that provides this type of empowerment and autonomy is a threat to an anti-democratic and authoritarian worldview like Christian Nationalism. No longer content to remove their children from public schools to shield them from information and values they disagree with, Christian Nationalists are now using the notion of "parental rights" to prevent public schools from preparing American students for life in a diverse, pluralistic republic. They insist that public schools not teach anything, including critical thinking itself, that may undermine their ability to transmit their political and religious worldview to their children. A minority faction of Christian Nationalists is now insisting that they have the right to use public schools to reinforce and promote their worldview.

While Christian Nationalists may oppose instruction aimed at developing individual autonomy because it equips students to critically reflect on their own inherited values and beliefs, they also oppose the promotion of civic virtue and concern for the common good as veiled attempts to endorse socialism. Civic virtue involves thinking about what will promote the general welfare of society and working to advance the common good. Often, exercising civic virtue requires the individual to transcend their personal self-interest and prioritize what is best for the community. It involves a willingness to place limits on individual freedom in the name of equal opportunity or equal protection. For many Christian Nationalists, individual rights should never be limited in the name of the common good and arguments in favor of doing so amount to a promotion of tyranny. Robert Reich, in *The Common Good*, describes the substance of a civic education that encourages civic virtue:

> It should explain and illustrate the profound differences between doing whatever it takes to win and acting for the common good; between getting as much as one can get for oneself and giving back to society; between assuming everyone is in it for themselves and understanding that we're all in it together; between seeking personal celebrity, wealth, or power and helping to build a better society for all.[40]

To Christian Nationalists, encouraging American students to "give back" or promote the "common good" is a way for liberal educators to defend the welfare state, progressive taxation, and limits on individual freedom. They reject the idea that individual freedom should ever be curbed in the interest of others, whether it involves taxation to fund public schools or face mask mandates to minimize the spread of a deadly virus. In other words, they believe that even if the majority agrees or will benefit, it does not justify limiting the freedom of the individual. That is, of course, unless Christian Nationalists believe they are the majority and should have the power to have their worldview reflected in the local public schools.

Christian Nationalism Infiltrates Suburban Houston

One of the largest school districts in Texas is in northwest Harris County in the suburbs of Houston. As a resident of the district and concerned parent, I began attending school board meetings in July 2021. I was immediately struck by the Christian Nationalist rhetoric being used by residents during the public comment portions of the meetings. That summer, what began as a relatively predictable conservative opposition to mask mandates and vaccines morphed into an often-incomprehensible obsession with the "threat" of Critical Race Theory (CRT). The parents who initially disrupted school board meetings to question the recommendations of public health experts became consumed by the prospect, always ridiculous and unfounded, that their children were being indoctrinated by progressive educators with the "woke" idea that all White people are "oppressors" and that they should feel shame and guilt for being White. This notion that children were being made to feel bad about the color of their skin became the genesis of a groundswell of opposition to CRT, which became the term for anything that discussed concepts of white privilege, systemic racism, or the legacy of white supremacy. One resident stated, "true Christ followers are horrified to learn how the CRT ideology and BLM have infiltrated many of our schools" and insisted that "things won't improve until we are more concerned about God's approval than the approval of the cult of CRT." Many of the attendees, duped into believing that young White children were being taught to feel shame about their race, gave her a standing ovation. The "Summer of CRT" would prove to be a turning point in the local school board elections taking place in November 2021.

In truth, the analytical framework known as Critical Race Theory was not being taught in the district or any K-12 public schools in Texas, but important discussions about privilege and the legacy of racism had begun to show up, appropriately, in some high school settings within the context of the nation's collective reckoning with racial injustice after George Floyd's murder. The propagandists of the GOP saw an opportunity to stoke White insecurity and inflame White resentment toward society's attempt to wrestle with deep questions about race. They funneled money into a faux grassroots movement against CRT in the hopes that it would inspire higher turnout of conservative voters at the polls. The architect of this plan was conservative activist Christopher Rufo who explained how Republicans could use CRT to divide communities for political purposes. This campaign of lies, as with previous warnings about the threat of "socialism" or "immigrant caravans" or "health care death panels," succeeded in many elections across Texas. What was unique, and more troubling, about the opposition to CRT was the role of Christian Nationalism and the direct threat it posed to public schools as the site where the principles and practices of pluralistic, democratic self-government are taught.

While school board races are nonpartisan, there were both Republicans and Democrats on the district's Board of Trustees, and residents were represented by both Republicans and Democrats in the Texas state legislature. Though the district does reflect some generalizations about suburbia in being mostly White and affluent in certain areas, it is also very economically and racially diverse in most parts of the district. In the wake of George Floyd's murder, the school board led with courage by adopting a "Resolution Condemning Racism." What seemed appropriate, if not benign in 2020, became "proof" of an agenda to indoctrinate students with CRT the following year. In 2021, three extremist candidates campaigned together for the Board of Trustees by opposing mask mandates, denouncing CRT, opposing LGBTQ+ inclusion, and signaling their Christian Nationalist worldview as the defenders of "parental rights."

Reading their campaign literature and listening to their public statements at campaign events, these extremists seemed to believe that anything that public schools teach or promote that contradicts what a parent believes is an attempt to indoctrinate children. They seemed totally oblivious to the fact that the diversity of values that parents hold within the community is equal to the diversity of the student population itself. They seemed to lack any comprehension of the civic purpose of public schools to prepare *everyone* for participation in our pluralistic, multicultural republic. To me, it was clear that they believed that their personal political and religious worldview should never be contradicted; or should even become the standard that is taught to everyone. In what are supposed to be nonpartisan campaigns, the three extremists ran openly as conservative Republicans. More alarming, they ran as Christians, and the community was bombarded with Christian Nationalist propaganda that only served to divide residents by introducing hostility, resentment, and mistrust into the community. Similar developments were taking place across Texas and the United States.

Campaign literature promoting the candidates declared, "We must take back the school boards that are controlled by the radical pro-Communist, anti-American leftists who are indoctrinating our children in Critical Race Theory and sexual perversion." The piece then stated, "We can change the direction of public education by electing conservative American Patriots to the school boards." The same campaign mailer encouraged the reader to "sign the Christian Patriot Declaration," which states:

> Stouthearted Christian Patriots must rise up to boldly oppose and defeat the domestic enemy forces of evil, the atheistic pro-Communist Democrats, the despicable baby killers, pornographers, pedophiles, sodomites, transgenders, Antifa, and the BLM that have infiltrated our civil government and threaten to destroy all vestiges of Biblical morality and U.S. Constitutional principles. These domestic enemies are traitors to God and country.[41]

The statement concludes, "Patriots, let's press this battle to restore our nation to its Christian heritage to its successful conclusion!" Again, this was campaign literature mailed to district residents on behalf of three school board candidates running for nonpartisan positions. The campaign mailers were sent by partisan groups like the Conservative Republicans of Harris County.

The three incumbents, two of which were conservative Republicans, tried their best to halt the Christian Nationalist offensive, but yard signs supporting the extremists started popping up all over town. I could feel what was coming like an inevitability. Their Christian Nationalism was on full display a few days before the election in a recorded interview that was posted on social media and YouTube. The video literally began with Christian praise music. During the discussion, the candidates made statements about gender based on their religious worldview that were demonstrably false. They claimed that Critical

Race Theory was developed by Karl Marx. They suggested that Martin Luther King Jr.'s dream that people be "judged by the content of their character, not the color of their skin" had been achieved. They all agreed with the idea that teachers should not have to "check their faith" at the door. They stated that educators "shouldn't have to pander to agendas" by using a student's preferred pronouns. One candidate said that he would recommend "never wearing a [face] mask" and called it "child abuse" to have children wear them. Every topic seemed to come back to "parental rights," as if the children themselves don't have rights or the ability to make their own decisions. It was clear that they resented the fact that public schools might equip students to think for themselves.

In the weeks before the election, they accused the district's Board of Trustees of engaging in "political theater" instead of focusing on student learning outcomes. In truth, the district had been singularly focused on student learning and responding to the challenges of the pandemic. The only political theater was that orchestrated at school board meetings by the minority faction of Christian Nationalists who heckled board members, interrupted speakers they disagreed with, and turned the room into what at times seemed like a political rally. Sitting in the room, I could see the beliefs and behaviors of liberal democracy slipping away. The Christian Nationalists had turned respectful and civil school board meetings into a circus and brought shame to the election process. They cynically exploited voters' fears and ignorance by riding an anti-CRT wave into office when Critical Race Theory was not even being taught in the district's public schools. Those leading the Christian Nationalist crusade are what Whitehead and Perry, in *Taking America Back for God*, label "Ambassadors."[42] According to their formula, Ambassadors, while being the strongest supporters of Christian Nationalism, are the smallest group. However, the largest group is the Accommodators, those who are susceptible to seeing the Ambassadors and their rhetoric in a positive light. In their quest to "save" students from the "threat" of CRT, a small group of Christian Nationalists (Ambassadors) were able to mobilize other residents (Accommodators) to elect three candidates whose public statements were at odds with the foundational values of the public school system and American republic: diversity, tolerance, pluralism, equal treatment, and freedom of thought. Two years later in 2023, three more extremists were elected to the Board of Trustees using the same tactics.

News of Christian Nationalism Spreads Across Texas

And it was not just in my local school district. The same tactics were being used in campaigns in other school districts across Texas and the United States. Awareness of the Christian Nationalist threat to Texas public schools slowly started to spread online. Former Granbury ISD school board trustee Chris Tackett and his wife Mendi Tackett produced a steady stream of content on Twitter and TikTok that served to identify the threat and inform voters from across the political spectrum. Frank Strong, an educator, took the initiative to chronicle the book bans taking place across the state. He used Twitter to share his "Book-Loving Texan's Guide" to inform residents about book bans and promote school board candidates opposed to such bans. Mike Hixenbaugh, an investigative reporter with NBC, produced numerous articles and two podcasts about the rise of Christian Nationalism in school districts across Texas. At times, it seemed like the pro-public education, and pro-democracy crowd was undergoing a crash course in Christian Nationalism and organizing to halt its advance. Alarmed by the electoral success of Christian Nationalism in my community, I founded a nonpartisan advocacy group in November 2021 after the school board election. We started out as a Facebook group and quickly grew to approximately 400 followers in a few weeks. Residents responded to the notion that the community needed a nonpartisan group that would promote strong, inclusive public schools that serve everyone. Our call to defend the foundational values of American society resonated with the community, and we started organizing on behalf of students, teachers, and families. We began speaking regularly at school board meetings, wrote emails to the district's leadership about important education issues, and delivered gifts to all librarians in the district when their professionalism and integrity were being attacked by state politicians. The work was difficult, but it felt relevant and rewarding.

Then, as quickly as CRT emerged as the biggest "threat" to students in public schools, it vanished from the conversation and was replaced by accusations of "pornography" in the libraries. The "porn" being described by Christian Nationalists at school board meetings was always a depiction of a same-sex romantic relationship. In the fall of 2021, Texas Governor Greg Abbott had instructed the Texas Education Agency to investigate "the availability of pornography"[43] in public school libraries, and Republican state representative Matt Krause had requested that Texas school districts report whether they had any of the books on a list of 850 texts that he insisted "might make students feel discomfort, guilt, anguish, or any other form of psychological distress because of their race or sex."[44] By the spring of 2022, the Christian Nationalists in my district and other districts across the state were insisting that books from Krause's list be removed from school libraries. Members of our nonpartisan advocacy group, including myself, who spoke out against book bans were called "groomers" online and at school board meetings and accused of sexualizing young children to make them more susceptible to sex trafficking. The attacks and insinuations were disgusting, especially since most of our group's members were parents with young children themselves. It was just the latest evidence of how destructive Christian Nationalism could be toward a democratic way of life. The parallels to the anti-communist hysteria of 1950s McCarthyism were hard to miss.

By the summer of 2022, the Christian Nationalists were so threatened by our nonpartisan activism on behalf of public schools that they created a rival group with the same name but trademarked it as an LLC. The new group's website described itself as a "Conservative Christian group that believes the Bible is the Word of God, Jesus Christ is Lord, and free volunteer service to others is a constructive way to help the community."[45] The group's Christian Nationalist identity and motivations were confirmed later that summer at a board meeting when one of their members announced an initiative to deliver "In God We Trust" signs to every campus in the district in accordance with a new state law. The bill was essentially a political stunt that weaponized Supreme Court rulings to permit Christian Nationalists to engage in "Culture War" theatrics. It mandates that any public school in Texas display a national motto sign if donated by a private entity. It allows Christian Nationalists, in their minds, to promote religion in schools by exploiting the fact that the U.S. Supreme Court has ruled that the national motto is secular in nature. The signs were paid for by The Yellow Rose of Texas Republican Women who stated on social media that "Students will have a visual reminder that our country has trusted in God since its founding." Never mind that the national motto only became "In God We Trust" in 1956 during the Cold War and that the republic's Founders coined the nation's first, and arguably more appropriate, motto "E Pluribus Unum" meaning "out of many, one."

Our nonpartisan group rebranded with a new name as an official 501(c)4 nonprofit in 2023. The group's vision is to "embrace the future, prioritize an inclusive and equitable learning environment, and support a diverse community where every child can thrive." We mobilized voters on behalf of nonpartisan school board candidates and helped form a coalition of Republicans, Independents, and Democrats committed to the idea that public schools must be inclusive and provide equal opportunity for all students. Public schools are where students of different classes, races, countries of origin, religions, and sexual orientations meet each other, learn empathy, and develop solidarity. The civic mission of public schools is to prepare all students for participation in America's diverse, pluralistic republic. Autonomy and civic virtue, the ability to think and choose one's values and life path, and identify one's well-being with the well-being of others, are the two pillars of a "vision of good citizenship" that can equip students to participate in democratic self-government and defend a democratic society. Christian Nationalists object to the civic mission of public schools because it undermines their movement to favor conservative Christianity and impose it on society.

Takeaways for Students and Parents

- Public schools are already teaching values, implicitly or explicitly, and students and parents must demand that they teach the values of liberal democracy.
- Students must organize and speak out about their education by demanding curriculum and instruction that affirm the beliefs and behaviors of a pluralistic society and democratic way of life.

- Parents must organize and speak out at school board meetings to denounce attempts by state lawmakers or school board trustees to ban books, silence educators, or create hostile learning environments.
- Parents must defend educators who are providing a civic education that cultivates empathy and solidarity by publicly or privately praising them to school administrators.
- Allowing Christian Nationalists to dominate the conversation is unacceptable. Leaders, from state capitols to school campuses, must hear from students and parents who care about the civic mission of public schools.
- Denouncing Christian Nationalism is not sufficient; the principles of liberal democracy must be celebrated and promoted.
- Students and parents must act as "Ambassadors" of liberal democracy to counteract the proponents of Christian Nationalism.

Notes

1. Richard Dagger, *Civic Virtues* (New York: Oxford University Press, 1997), 197.
2. William Galston, *Liberal Purposes* (Cambridge: Cambridge University Press, 1991), 79.
3. Ibid., 44.
4. Ibid., 6.
5. Ibid., 220.
6. Ibid.
7. Amy Gutmann, *Democratic Education* (Princeton: Princeton University Press, 1987), 39.
8. Ibid.
9. Thomas Spragens, *Civic Liberalism* (Lanham: Rowman and Littlefield, 1999), xvi.
10. Ibid., 123.
11. William Galston, "Two Concepts of Liberalism," *Ethics* 105, no. 3 (April 1995): 522.
12. Ibid., 523.
13. Gutmann, *Democratic Education*, 44.
14. Ibid.
15. Dagger, *Civic Virtues*, 30.
16. Ibid.
17. Ibid.
18. Ibid., 38.
19. Ibid., 194.
20. Spragens, *Civic Liberalism*, 116.
21. Ibid.
22. Ibid., 121.
23. Ibid., 125.
24. Ibid., 129.
25. Dagger, *Civic Virtues*, 196.
26. Spragens, *Civic Liberalism*, 235.

27 Ibid.
28 Ibid.
29 Ibid.
30 Dagger, *Civic Virtues*, 117.
31 Ibid., 112.
32 Ibid., 118.
33 Andrew Peterson, *Civic Republicanism and Civic Education* (Basingstoke: Palgrave Macmillan, 2011), 1.
34 Ibid., 3.
35 Ibid., 13.
36 Ibid., 3.
37 Peter Levine and Ann Higgins-D'Alessandro "The Philosophical Foundations of Civic Education," *Philosophy and Public Policy Quarterly* 30, no. 3/4 (December 2010): 21.
38 Ibid.
39 "Support for Same-Sex Marriage at Record High, but Key Segments Remain Opposed," *Pew Research Center*, June 8, 2015.
40 Robert Reich, *The Common Good* (New York: Knopf, 2018), 178–179.
41 www.crtpac.com.
42 Andrew L. Whitehead and Samuel L. Perry, *Taking America Back for God: Christian Nationalism in the United States* (New York: Oxford University Press, 2020), 37.
43 Kate McGee, "Texas Critical Race Theory Bill Limiting Teaching of Current Events Signed into Law," June 15, 2021, www.texastribune.org.
44 Bill Chappell, "A Texas Lawmaker Is Targeting 850 Books That He Says Could Make Students Feel Uneasy," October 28, 2021, www.npr.org.
45 www.cypressfps.org.

4 The Root of the Problem

Liberal Democracy's Neutrality

In *Democracy's Discontent*, political theorist Michael Sandel states that "the relativist defense of liberalism is no defense at all."[1] His claim is made in the context of describing, and criticizing, the "neutrality" that often characterizes the liberal democratic society of the United States. He provides a summary of liberal neutrality, stating:

> since people disagree about the best way to live, government should not affirm in law any particular vision of the good life. Instead, it should provide a framework of rights that respects persons as free and independent selves, capable of choosing their own values and ends.[2]

As discussed in previous chapters, many political theorists deny that public schools can remain neutral when providing civic education, and it is arguably not desirable to do so in the face of anti-democratic threats such as Christian Nationalism. A liberal republic like the United States must promote the values of liberal democracy and republican self-government to preserve itself. Sandel is one of many political theorists invested in reviving the republican tradition to strengthen liberal democracy. As he sees it, "republican politics cannot be neutral toward the values and ends its citizens espouse. The republican conception of freedom . . . requires a formative politics, a politics that cultivates in citizens the qualities of character self-government requires."[3]

In the previous chapter, we surveyed the attempts by political theorists to identify the qualities of character and citizenship necessary to preserve liberal democracy and participate in a democratic society. I have made the argument, which political theorists have also recognized, that the qualities of good citizenship may be practically indistinguishable from a "vision of the good life." While the liberal republic that Sandel describes is reluctant to endorse a "vision of the good life" because it violates individual autonomy, I believe it is now necessary to promote a normative "vision of good citizenship" to combat the illiberal and authoritarian threat of Christian Nationalism. While the public school system

DOI: 10.4324/9781032686059-4

may claim, or attempt, to not promote specific values, it must be conceded that "toleration and freedom and fairness are values too, and they can hardly be defended by the claim that no values can be defended."[4] In other words, whether American public schools are currently promoting the values of liberal democracy or not, they *should* be. The emphasis on "neutrality" to respect individual rights has allowed individuals to discriminate against others in the name of religious freedom and promote anti-democratic agendas at odds with the liberalism that protects individual rights in the first place. Sadly, American public schools have become evidence of liberalism's tendency to allow illiberalism to flourish.

While American public schools seemed to be making progress on the promotion of tolerance and inclusion, the excessive individualism of America's liberal society has enabled a minority faction to denounce and silence perspectives they disagree with. For example, a school district may have had success with a program such as No Place for Hate, which is sponsored by the Anti-Defamation League, but a loud minority of parents can get the entire program canceled because it supposedly violates their political or religious worldview. In this way, Christian Nationalism makes its influence felt by preventing everyone's children from learning about tolerance and inclusion because doing so contradicts the political and religious values of one group of parents. The individual's supposed freedom to not have government undermine their family's values is used to take away other people's individual freedom to learn values they do agree with. Again, the Christian Nationalist worldview that motivates opposition to a program like No Place for Hate could reflect the views of a minority or majority in the community, but in either case, it is inappropriate for the values of liberal democracy to not be taught simply because it offends people with anti-democratic and intolerant beliefs.

The public school system belongs to the community as a whole, and its civic mission requires it to prepare students for participation in a diverse, pluralistic republic. Christian Nationalists increasingly try to claim that public schools belong to them by making appeals to their status as taxpayers and arguments that America was founded as a "Christian nation." What seems to be forgotten, or not acknowledged, is that other families also pay taxes and may practice a different faith tradition or none. Too many parents seem to believe that if something is public, then it shouldn't contradict anything that is private. They essentially argue that it is wrong or corrupt or oppressive for their tax dollars to teach values that contradict their own. It makes absolutely no sense for any family to expect the instruction of public schools to be entirely compatible with whatever political or religious worldview they teach at home. The public schools serve the entire population, and the content of what is taught should reflect the range of diversity that exists in the population. If parents want to teach specific values to their children about reproduction, sexual identity, gender roles, American history, or anything else, then they can do so in their homes or churches. Parents should not have the right to impose their political and religious worldview on everyone else by silencing teachers or removing aspects of the curriculum they disagree with.

In the past, if conservative Christian parents objected to the local public schools because they did not reflect their family's values, then they would homeschool or send their children to private Christian schools. Parallel systems of education have existed for decades wherein students are taught explicitly Christian-centric versions of American history, science, and other subjects like health. Still, the values of those opposed to the civic mission of public schools have long impacted public schools themselves. For example, health in Texas is not required in high school and still uses an abstinence-only approach to sex education. In a social studies classroom, the emphasis has been on presenting "both sides" of an issue or including a variety of perspectives on a topic. For example, when students in Texas public schools learn about the Civil War, they study the inaugural addresses of American President Abraham Lincoln *and* Confederate President Jefferson Davis. The result is a mischaracterization of what motivated secessionists and the perpetuation of the narrative that "states' rights" was the main underlying cause of the conflict. In this way, teaching "both sides" is used to counteract a narrative that conservative Christians do not like. Still, in other contexts, conservative Christians regard teaching "both sides" as having a bias against a conservative Christian worldview. Teaching students how to look at an issue from a variety of perspectives is controversial because competing views are presented as equally valid. For Christian Nationalists, truth, whether it is about religion, politics, history, or sex, is absolute, and any instruction that acknowledges that truth is contested, or a matter of perspective, is seen as an attempt to undermine the family's values.

In situation after situation, conservative Christians perceive a "bias" against their values and then insist on a "balanced" approach that favors their worldview. In my experience as an educator and observer of events in Texas, conservative Christians view anything that does not promote or reinforce a conservative Christian worldview as biased against them. In their attempt to replace what is "biased" with something that is "fair," they typically introduce actual bias where none existed before. They identify something as having a "liberal" or "progressive" bias, then seek to insert a "conservative" replacement. In other words, they do not actually have an objection to bias; they simply insist that the bias be in their favor. The truth is that American public schools do remain largely "neutral" on divisive issues, but for conservative Christians, this neutrality is "biased" against their worldview. Or, if the schools are not strictly speaking "neutral" and instead teach "both sides," then conservative parents often consider that even worse because their children are being given possible alternatives to what they teach at home. In the face of all this political and parental pressure, it is clear why public schools have gradually stopped talking about or teaching anything remotely controversial, contemporary, or contested. At the national, state, and local levels, the message is being sent by Christian

Nationalists that educators need to promote a conservative Christian worldview or keep their mouths shut. Too many administrators, bowing to the demands of parents, are throwing their teachers under the bus and enabling the slow-motion capture of the public school's civic mission.

Teaching Lies to Teach the Truth

The election of Donald Trump in 2016 was a challenging development for many civic educators. Not only was Trump objectively unfit for office from the perspective of many political scientists, but he also won in an indecent and undemocratic manner having made a mockery of the election process itself and received a minority of the popular vote. For those knowledgeable about our constitutional system and concerned about its health, every week of Trump's presidency brought a new existential threat to the separation of powers, checks and balances, the rule of law, and the values of liberal democracy. It was as if the school-yard bully had become principal of the school. Teaching social studies, specifically U.S. History and American Government, became more difficult during Trump's time in office. I started to get anonymous and threatening emails from parents who thought I was too "liberal" in the classroom. Lessons and discussions that received zero pushback prior to 2016 received lots of scrutiny after Trump's election.

Administrators in my building referred to anonymous parent emails denigrating my character and integrity as "data." I received hate mail at my home address. I was constantly walking on a tightrope trying to provide my students with a meaningful civic education without inviting the wrath of their parents. It was exhausting. Teaching is a thankless enough job without being viewed as some sinister influence corrupting the youth of the community. At one point, an administrator asked me what I was doing to invite the anonymous parent complaints, which to me was like asking a woman what she did to attract sexual harassment. I wasn't doing anything other than my job, which involved using my knowledge of history and political science to contextualize current events and facilitate the development of critical thinking skills.

Like many teachers in the K-12 system, I was starting to get burned out. In my 20s, I had been young and idealistic enough to "fight the good fight" in the face of external and internal pressure, but as the Trump presidency continued, I started looking for an exit. One of the turning points for me involved a dispute over an instructional resource for a dual-credit (community college) course being taught within the high school. On my campus, we blended dual-credit and advanced placement students into a single class. In other words, I had students preparing to take the College Board's AP examination and students earning a college credit through a partnership with the local community college. From the college's perspective, they expected the course to be taught like a college class despite being in a high school. From the high school's perspective, they expected to retain control over the curriculum and instructional materials used within their building. It was common, if not required, for dual-credit and

AP classes to use a secondary text in addition to the standard textbook. I had been using Robert Dahl's *On Democracy* for a few years but decided to introduce a new text for the 2017–2018 school year that dealt with a more specific and contemporary issue: voting rights.

I had read Ari Berman's *Give Us the Ballot: The Modern Struggle for Voting Rights in America*, published in 2015, and decided that it was a great text that combined history, policymaking, judicial interpretation, and current events. I spoke to my liaison at the community college about the text, and they were ecstatic about how engaging the text would be in the context of the recent *Shelby County v. Holder (2013)* decision, new state laws to combat supposed voter fraud, and President Trump's "Election Integrity Commission." The text was rich in content and connections to the curriculum standards. I worked on the assignments, reading schedule, and essay prompts in June and July; then in August, I informed my department chair at the high school that I would be using a different secondary text for the new school year. Surprisingly, I was told that my book would need to be approved by an administrator, which was odd, because there had been no approval or review process for the previous book. Admittedly, Ari Berman is progressive, but the book itself was well researched, and any of the more partisan claims about whether voter fraud was a real threat or not could be presented to students as contested claims. I became nervous that there was going to be pushback, because of either the topic or the partisan identity of the author.

The administrator who "reviewed" the book sent me an email asking if I could indicate which TEKS (Texas's content standards) the text aligned with. I considered this a definite red flag, but politely played the game. I sent a 6- to 8-page document explaining how the text aligned with the TEKS, College Board curriculum, and community college learning objectives. Then, things got interesting fast. After conceding that the book clearly aligned with curriculum standards, the administrator expressed concern that the book had a liberal/ progressive bias and that our *community* would not approve of it. I was shocked than an administrator would state in writing that an instructional resource aligned with curriculum standards but could not be used due to the political views of my students' parents. Trying to seem reasonable, he then stated that unless the "other side" of the issue could be presented, then the book was not approved.

Most of the book is simply a historical narrative of the Voting Rights Act's passage and implementation. In other words, the history of voter discrimination and racism just is what it is. As for Berman's commentary about current events, which included skepticism that voter fraud was a real problem and criticism of Republican-led states, like Texas, for passing laws making it more difficult to register and cast a ballot, it seemed somehow impractical to present "both sides" of the issue. What was the other side? Lies about non-existent voter fraud threatening elections. Attempts to make it harder, in the words of federal district court judges, for racial minorities and college students to vote. Did I really have to lend credibility to the side fear mongering about voter fraud to inform students about the *real* threat of voter suppression after the Supreme Court gutted the Voting Rights Act in 2013?

Since I had already done all the preparation to integrate the book into my course and believed in principle that it was inappropriate for an instructional resource to be denied on such grounds, I decided to call the administrator's bluff and found a book that represented the "other side." It was *Who's Counting: How Fraudsters and Bureaucrats Put Your Vote at Risk* by John Fund and Hans von Spakovky. It was a hack job compared to Berman's historical research, and one of the authors was appointed to serve on Trump's "Election Integrity Commission." The lies and propaganda from the "other side" would now have a platform in my classroom. I told myself this was just the price of doing business, but it did not seem fair because *Who's Counting* was far more biased than *Give Us the Ballot*. It would be like hosting a forum on gun violence and having to invite Alex Jones to speak because you invited representatives from Everytown for Gun Safety or Moms Demand Action. In this instance, teaching "both sides" seemed to give credibility to lies, misinformation, and conspiracy theories. Still, I believed in the importance of the topic, and I wanted to do the work. The administrator was not happy that I called their bluff. They responded (all this correspondence was via email) that I would not be using *Give Us the Ballot* under any circumstances. I explained to my liaison at the community college what was going on, and they became irate that a college class was being micro-managed by a high school administrator. At this point, I was caught in the middle, and the dispute went above my pay grade.

In the end, the administrator, possibly realizing the hole they had dug by putting all their correspondence in writing, agreed to review *Who's Counting* and approved the use of both texts for the upcoming school year. As the approval process took place at the high school, news of the incident apparently made its way to the school district's superintendent and the president of the community college. I tried to be as clear as I could that I was not taking sides with either campus, and just wanted policy to be clarified. There was simply no way, as some at the college insisted, that a dual-credit instructor should have total discretion to teach whatever they wanted because the course was a college class. At the same time, it was inappropriate for the high school to insist that certain resources could not be used because they contradicted the political views of some parents. As a dual-credit instructor, I was teaching in an environment with overlapping jurisdictions, and it seemed unsustainable. After all, a class simply is not a college class if teachers can have instructional materials rejected over concerns about what parents will say. College is for adults who can think for themselves. The last I heard, the district superintendent and college president were going to discuss the viability of the entire dual-credit partnership; then, Hurricane Harvey brought days of relentless rain that literally flooded both the high school and the community college campuses. Suddenly, everyone had bigger problems to solve, and I proceeded to teach "both sides" of the issue. What was the bigger problem: voter suppression or voter fraud? I started to think that the root of the problem was much bigger.

From Teaching Both Sides to Picking Sides

The New York Times Magazine began releasing essays from *The 1619 Project* in August 2019 to discuss the legacy of slavery in American history. The project "aims to reframe the country's history by placing the consequences of slavery and the contributions of black Americans at the very center of our national narrative."[5] I remember reading some of the essays at the time and thinking they were very powerful and engaging. I could see how useful the materials could be in an American history course. Much as Howard Zinn's *A People's History of the United States* had been used to include alternative perspectives on well-known historical events, it seemed like *The 1619 Project* could be used to think differently about the American Founding's paradoxes and contradictions. No history teacher ever used Zinn's book as a comprehensive narrative of American history. It was always used in conjunction with traditional textbooks. Similarly, *The 1619 Project* was never intended to replace standard accounts of the American Founding, but conservative Republican lawmakers found the work's argument so threatening that they started to ban its use in classrooms across the country. Clearly, an honest consideration of the history of slavery complicates and undermines a Christian Nationalist version of American history and calls into question claims about American exceptionalism. From an educator's perspective, the policy shift was clear and unmistakable. It was no longer tolerable for educators to teach "both sides" of an issue. According to Christian Nationalist activists and lawmakers, the side represented by *The 1619 Project* needed to be silenced and banned. Only one side, the Christian Nationalist viewpoint, would be permitted.

In June 2021, the Texas legislature moved to ban the use of *The 1619 Project* in classrooms with House Bill 3979. The bill was described as an "anti-CRT" bill and was similar to legislation passed in other states after the national reckoning over discrimination and racism that followed the murder of George Floyd in 2020. The country, and its classrooms, were grappling with the realities of injustice, and the response from Christian Nationalists was to restrict the discussion of slavery, white supremacy, or any aspect of American history that might make White students experience discomfort or guilt. At the same time that Texas was accusing *The 1619 Project* of an anti-American or unpatriotic bias, it was passing House Bill 2497 to create the 1836 Project Advisory Committee to promote a patriotic version of Texas history that highlights Texas's exceptionalism.

The response followed a familiar formula: denounce something for being biased against conservatism or Christianity, attempt to ban it, and then replace it with something that overtly promotes a conservative or Christian worldview. The 1836 Project Advisory Committee is led by the president of the conservative Heritage Foundation and others with a documented history of promoting ideological versions of Texas history.[6] Fortunately, the materials produced by the 1836 Project are not intended for public school classrooms, but instead as pamphlets available when residents obtain or renew their driver's license. In August 2022, *Texas Monthly* published a detailed analysis of the 1836 Project's work and concluded that "the sanitized and whitewashed history state leaders wish to dispense to us along with our driver's licenses is nothing more than a deceitful propaganda effort that discredits the history profession."[7]

The inspiration for the 1836 Project was Donald Trump's 1776 Commission, which was created days before the 2020 election and called for a "pro-American" history curriculum to counteract indoctrination by "anti-American" progressives and liberals. The 1776 Commission issued its report in January 2021 as Trump was leaving the White House and "drew intense criticism from historians, some of whom noted that the commission, while stocked with conservative educators, did not include a single professional historian of the United States."[8] The report is full of declarations promoting civic education and good citizenship, but conservative Christian assumptions permeate the document. American history and politics are presented from an essentially Christian Nationalist standpoint that reinterprets past injustice and discrimination as something that Americans heroically overcame instead of something they willfully perpetuated and promoted. Reading the report, it is as if a conservative Republican sat down and reimagined a past where any wrongs that did exist were righted by conservatives and any contemporary threats to the country come from progressives. Slavery? Yes, it happened, but conservatives abolished it. Identity politics? Yes, progressives keep trying to divide Americans by always talking about the legacy of slavery and white supremacy.

As a social studies teacher from Texas, the 1776 Commission's report doesn't read that differently from the state's current social studies curriculum standards or textbooks. The American founding is presented as a crusade for individual rights and limited government. The American Founders are all characterized as Christians who believed Christianity was central to the nation's founding. The supposed separation of church and state is primarily about government not interfering with religious liberty. The growth in government power in the 19th and 20th centuries was a betrayal of the American Founding, and progressivism is a slippery slope to socialism and tyranny. The report is a conservative Christian version of American history, and it is the version of American history that Christian Nationalists wanted to be taught in public schools across the country. Again, having taught social studies in Texas, I can confirm that the curriculum already has a plenty of conservative Christian bias, but even so, if a teacher tries to teach "both sides" by including resources like *The 1619 Project*, then they are accused of indoctrination. It seems that calls to teach "both sides" are used to include conservative views where the impression is that only liberal views are represented, but if given the chance, conservatives are more than happy to "pick sides" by silencing alternative views to their own.

Additional evidence that teaching "both sides" is being replaced by "picking sides" is the development of an overtly Christian Nationalist homeschool curriculum. On its website, *The Christendom Curriculum* describes itself as "America's only Christian Nationalist homeschool curriculum" that "rejects the globalist and social justice warrior demand to despise our American and Western history, heritage, and heroes."[9] The website insists that the curriculum is "completely free of Woke ideology." *The Christendom Curriculum* is a comprehensive pre-K through high school curriculum that, according to its creator, "openly and boldly addresses the major civilizational crisis of our time . . . and trains young people to engage in the Culture War with a view toward long-term victory." While this homeschool curriculum may seem like an obscure or fringe set of instructional materials, private Christian schools across America can quickly adopt similar curriculums that effectively indoctrinate students to be hostile toward the separation of church and state, religious pluralism, multiculturalism, and equality for the LGBTQ+ community. In fact, elected officials in Oklahoma are already promoting a Christianity-focused history curriculum for public schools[10] and recently approved the first religious public charter school in the country.

What begins as a homeschool resource can quickly be adopted by private Christian schools and then promoted by Christian Nationalist politicians for public schools. In this way, fringe ideas circulating within the Christian homeschooling community can quickly migrate to private schools and then public schools. Furthermore, the Texas State Board of Education does not need to formally approve instructional resources for educators to draw inspiration from them. Now that the term Christian Nationalism has been formalized, it will be much easier for those who adhere to a Christian Nationalist worldview to unite around a shared political vision and policy agenda. The author of *The Christendom Curriculum* explains that because "[w]e believe in *Christendom:* Christ's rule over the nations . . . we are compelled to embrace what is now called Christian Nationalism, and to reject its opposite, Globalism."[11] In other words, Christian Nationalists are acting with intention and consciously preparing the next generation to implement a Christian Nationalist agenda. There is nothing to prevent churches or non-profits from offering free professional development to educators that provides access to Christian Nationalist instructional resources.

Further evidence for the potential of public schools to be remade in the image of private Christian schools is the role that Hillsdale College has played in promoting an overtly conservative curriculum in charter schools in states like Florida. Before Florida was in the news for objecting to the College Board's new African American studies course and legislation that targeted LGBTQ+ teachers, the state embraced the growth of charter schools that use a conservative curriculum produced by Hillsdale College, a private Christian college in Michigan.[12] The rationale is familiar and demonstrates the true motivations of Christian Nationalist critics of public education. Accusations of "liberal" or "woke" bias are leveled against public schools, which then intimidates administrators and educators to appear more "neutral" by teaching "both sides" or ignoring anything political or controversial at all; then, an overtly conservative curriculum with actual bias is offered as an alternative. Again, the problem does not seem to be bias itself, but simply having the *wrong* bias.

The Hillsdale College curriculum spread to Texas in 2023 after the State Board of Education voted to approve a new charter school called Heritage

Classical Academy in northwest Houston. According to its website, Heritage Classical Academy will use the Hillsdale College "Barney Charter School" curriculum, which includes the "1776 Curriculum" that shares the ideological assumptions of the 1776 Commission created by Donald Trump. Additionally, the conservative nonprofit PragerU, which makes educational videos and content, has aggressively marketed its materials in Florida and Texas. Videos produced by PragerU have a striking conservative bias and may become common-place supplemental materials in classrooms where teachers opt to promote a conservative worldview. These examples demonstrate that calls to teach "both sides" are a subtle way to create the space to ultimately "take sides."

When the Texas legislature passes a law like HB 3979, which requires teachers to discuss "both sides" of contemporary or controversial events, it gradually introduces the idea that there is no objective morality or historical truth. Christian Nationalists can then use the existing relativism as a means to introduce their absolutist worldview. The result was evident in Carroll ISD when the district's director of curriculum and instruction told teachers that they needed to provide the "opposing" perspective when teaching or talking about the Holocaust.[13] Likewise, one can only assume that according to this logic, teachers would need to mention Putin's perspective on the Russian invasion of Ukraine or the insurrectionists perspective on the January 6, 2021, attack on the U.S. Capitol. In other words, the Christian Nationalist accusation that everything is biased is used as cover for the introduction of bias where little or no bias previously existed.

Christian Nationalists are picking sides by openly embracing curriculum that has a conservative Christian bias. They seem to justify doing so by claiming that they are leveling the playing field or teaching the truth. The assumption is that schools, whether K-12 or colleges, have long had a liberal bias so it is justified to fight fire with fire and promote a conservative bias. The problem, in my view as an educator, is that the supposed liberal bias is never as striking as the conservative bias that is introduced. In other words, the solution to the problem is too strong, and the medicine, far from healing an illness, introduces one instead. It is a remarkable thing to denounce public schools for having a liberal bias and then knowingly introduce a conservative bias to replace it. From the Christian Nationalist standpoint, what was nefarious before is now seen as redemptive.

Christian Nationalism is an ideology of absolute truth, and its proponents feel it is their duty to God to spread the truth. In this situation, civic education stands paralyzed at a crossroads: some educators, sensing the need to preserve liberal democracy, want to double-down on the promotion of democratic values; others are caught in the difficult task of teaching "both sides," which may require them to give credibility to falsehoods and *still* exposes them to accusations of bias for presenting competing worldviews or values as equally valid. Christian Nationalists, having helped to create the division and confusion, then offer another path: an overtly Christian Nationalist curriculum that promotes conservative Christianity.

Laboratories of Christian Nationalism

In Texas, Lieutenant Governor Dan Patrick spearheaded an effort to create a new conservative think tank at The University of Texas-Austin to combat what he felt was liberal bias within the university. The think tank, initially called the Liberty Institute, was to be "dedicated to the study and teaching of individual liberty, limited government, private enterprise and free markets."[14] The institute was ultimately renamed the Civitas Institute and its website states that

> liberal education is at once a liberating education and a quest for wisdom about how to live well. Such a liberating education is indispensable for future civic leaders, who are the custodians of the American polity, and it rests on open inquiry, reasoned debate, civil discussion, and freedom of thought and speech.[15]

The mission statement for the program is wonderful, but it does not differ meaningfully from the mission statement of any other liberal arts education, including existing programs at The University of Texas-Austin.

Christian Nationalists and conservative Republican lawmakers accuse the K-12 public school system and higher education institutions of liberal indoctrination, but one reason that college may seem so "liberal" to some students is the fact that the K-12 system *already* has a somewhat "conservative" bias. In Texas, for example, the state curriculum standards for social studies, science, and health are all determined by a majority of conservative Republicans on the State Board of Education. Additional laws governing public education in the state are passed by conservative Republican majorities in the state legislature. The purpose of an education, especially higher education, is to empower students to think for themselves, which involves exposure to competing perspectives and worldviews. An education is not good, right, or fair based on the conclusions that students come to when presented with choices about what to believe. In the marketplace of ideas, conservatives often lose because people disagree with conservative ideas.

Clearly, conservative Christians believe that they are losing because the public education system is biased against them. Presumably, they tell themselves that if students reject a conservative Christian worldview, then something is wrong with the curriculum and instruction. That is why teaching "both sides" is no longer sufficient to rebut claims of indoctrination and why denunciations of liberal bias are simultaneous with the promotion of conservative bias. The Christian Nationalist rejection of American public schools on the grounds that they promote inclusion for the LGBTQ+ community and equal treatment and opportunity for everyone regardless of race or religion is coupled with the promotion of "classical" charter schools that use an overtly conservative Christian curriculum created by Hillsdale College. Likewise, Christian Nationalist objections to colleges and universities discussing the threat of climate change, grappling with the history of racism and discrimination, and promoting the common good are coupled with the creation of overtly conservative think tanks and programs that prioritize individual liberty over equality and characterize any new government program or regulation as a socialist threat to capitalism.

While Texas Lieutenant Governor Dan Patrick's Liberty Institute may not in its current form be as ideologically strident as he had hoped, the push to create overtly conservative spaces and programs at Texas colleges and universities continues. In 2023, West Texas A&M University in the Texas Panhandle announced the creation of the Hill Institute to teach and promote "West Texas values." Patrick, attending the event that announced the initiative, stated that "This is the America that all America used to be, it should be again."[16] According to the *Texas Tribune*, Patrick then suggested to the chancellor of Texas A&M University System that he would like to help establish similar institutes across the entire system, stating, "We need to turn our face back to God. Stand on that foundation."[17] Such brazen Christian Nationalist rhetoric and conservative bias is not confined to the Lone Star State. In the case of Florida's New College, a small liberal arts school, Governor Ron DeSantis simply stacked the board of trustees with conservative ideologues who openly pushed a conservative worldview to alter the entire campus's identity.[18]

The Christian Nationalist response to progressive "indoctrination" on college campuses or a lack of intellectual diversity is to impose a Christian Nationalist agenda and mandate intellectual conformity to conservative principles. The response is authoritarian and evokes the famous quote from George Orwell's *1984*: "Who controls the past controls the future. Who controls the present control the past." Christian Nationalists are using the levers of power at the state and local level to impose their illiberal worldview on society. In states like Florida and Texas, they are attempting to use raw power to indoctrinate the next generation with conservative Christian values. Even if Christian Nationalists fall short of their goal to fundamentally transform the public school system, they have already succeeded in constructing a highly ideological parallel system of charter schools and private schools that will prepare a not insignificant portion of the next generation to fight the Culture War on behalf of conservative Christianity. In some instances, it appears that a literal army of Christian Nationalists is being built.

In Fredericksburg, Texas, the Patriot Academy offers courses to 16- to 25-year-olds in "Biblical, Historical, and Constitutional principles"[19] as part of their Leadership Congress. Testimonials from participants describe being prepared to fight today's Culture Wars to defend liberty from socialism. The Patriot Academy campus also includes a "Constitutional Defense Center" that provides firearm instruction. Another testimonial described the belief, after attending Patriot Academy's Leadership Congress, in the ability of a "small army" to change the world. Private institutions like the Patriot Academy demonstrate that Christian Nationalists, while currently posing a threat to public schools, do not have to succeed in their conquest of them to threaten liberal democracy. Even if the public school system is saved from Christian Nationalism, plenty of students will attend camps, programs, and retreats designed to radicalize them with notions that American government and society must be saved by conservative Christians. The fact that Patriot Academy makes an explicit link between teaching a conservative interpretation of the U.S. Constitution and firearm instruction referred to as "constitutional defense" is disturbing and alarming. It's as if the far-right militia movement is being integrated with a Christian Nationalist curriculum and marketed to conservative parents as the necessary antidote to the supposed "woke" indoctrination the local public school is imposing on their child.

Christian Nationalists and their Republican political allies have picked sides. No longer supportive of the "neutral" liberal state characterized by a separation of church and state and religious pluralism, or the notion of teaching "both sides" and allowing students to think for themselves, Christian Nationalists have chosen to abandon the fundamental values of liberal democracy in favor of an authoritarian worldview. The premise of this book is that the defenders of liberal democracy, which includes *many* conservative Christians who do not identify with Christian Nationalism, must heed the warning: "fundamentalists rush in where liberals fear to tread."[20] Those who believe in equal treatment and opportunity, in freedom of expression and thought, and religious diversity and pluralism, must unite across political, racial, and religious lines to defend the civic mission of America's public schools.

Those who believe in liberal democracy must demand a public school system that prepares the next generation for participation in America's diverse, pluralistic republic. Furthermore, it is imperative that Christian Nationalists should not be permitted to co-opt the concepts of civic virtue and civic education. Goodness is *not* synonymous with the Western tradition, conservatism, or Christianity. Freedom is *not* simply rugged individualism, low taxes, or access to firearms. Currently, Christian Nationalists are offering a particular vision of civic education that they insist will revitalize America but that may, in fact, threaten its very foundations. Americans who believe in the liberal principles of representative democracy must construct and offer an alternative "vision of good citizenship." A normative civic education that unapologetically promotes the values of liberal democracy does *not* mean embracing a "woke" agenda. Public schools should not aim to cultivate good Christians *or* good Progressives. America's public schools should aim to produce good humans who see the intrinsic value of a democratic way of life. Doing so will require taking the side of liberal democracy over authoritarianism.

Takeaways for Educators

- Educators must shrewdly navigate state and local attempts to introduce a conservative Christian bias into curriculum, instruction, and school culture.

- Educators must find a way, whether through teaching "both sides" or "taking sides," to promote the beliefs and behaviors of liberal democracy.
- Educators must organize and speak out against attempts to undermine their professionalism, expertise, and integrity.
- Denouncing Christian Nationalism is not sufficient; the principles of liberal democracy must be celebrated and promoted.
- Educators must act as "Ambassadors" of liberal democracy to counteract the proponents of Christian Nationalism.

Notes

1. Michael Sandel, *Democracy's Discontent* (Cambridge: Harvard University Press, 1998), 8.
2. Ibid., 4.
3. Ibid., 6.
4. Ibid., 8.
5. *1619 Project*, www.nytimes.com/interactive/2019/08/14/magazine/1619-america-slavery.html.
6. Leah Lagrone and Michael Phillips, "What the 1836 Project Leaves Out in Its Version of Texas History," *Texas Monthly*, August 25, 2022.
7. Lagrone and Phillips, "What the 1836 Project Leaves Out in Its Version of Texas History."
8. Michael Crowley and Jennifer Schuessler, "Trump's 1776 Commission Critiques Liberalism in Report Derided by Historians," *New York Times*, January 20, 2021.
9. *The Christendom Curriculum*, www.christendomcurriculum.com.
10. Janelle Stecklein, "Oklahoma Education Official Pushing for Christianity-Centered History Curriculum," *The Joplin Globe*, October 30, 2022.
11. *The Christendom Curriculum*, www.christendomcurriculum.com.
12. Stephanie Saul, "A College Fights 'Leftist Academics' by Expanding into Charter Schools," *New York Times*, April 11, 2022.
13. Mike Hixenbaugh and Antonia Hylton, "Southlake School Leader Tells Teachers to Balance Holocaust Books with 'Opposing' Views," *NBC News*, October 15, 2021.
14. Kate McGee, "Professors Behind Conservative-Backed Liberty Institute Say UT Has Strayed from Plan," *The Texas Tribune*, June 8, 2022.
15. *Civitas Institute*, https://civitas.utexas.edu.
16. Kate McGee, "West Texas A&M University Receives $20 Million Gift for New Institute to Promote Texas Panhandle Values," *Texas Tribune*, October 4, 2023.
17. Ibid.
18. Kathryn Joyce, "The Florida of Today Is the America of Tomorrow: Ron DeSantis's New College Takeover Is Just the Beginning of the Right's Higher Ed Crusade," *Vanity Fair*, February 10, 2023.
19. *Patriot Academy*, www.patriotacademy.com.
20. Michael Sandel, *Justice* (New York: Farrar, Straus and Giroux, 2009), 243.

5 A Republic, If We Teach It

The Perfectionist Rationale for Civic Education

Having considered the possible content of a normative civic education and established that taking sides against Christian Nationalism is necessary, it is important to evaluate the rationale for embracing a robust defense of liberal democracy. It is clear that public schools are already engaged to some degree in taking sides on normative questions about how to live, and it is obvious that Christian Nationalists have no qualms taking sides and promoting their political and religious worldview, but what is the proper role of government in providing civic education if the content of "good citizenship" is arguably the content of the "good life"? If, as Sandel and others have argued, the government in a liberal democracy is supposed to remain neutral on how to live, then on what grounds can a liberal democracy promote a normative civic education? So far, the argument in favor of a normative civic education that promotes a "vision of good citizenship" has been grounded in the need to protect liberal democracy from authoritarian threats like Christian Nationalism, but is such an instrumental justification the strongest rationale? Does it make sense to teach something merely in the service of a stable and healthy political system?

I contend that it is appropriate and necessary for a liberal democracy like the United States to regard a democratic way of life as the "good life" and the small-d democratic citizen as a "good human." Republican theorists such as Sandel, writing in the tradition of Aristotle, insist that civic virtue is intrinsically good for the individual because political participation itself is considered part of the "good life." Aristotle provides a "vision of the good life" with a single end in mind, political participation, which is what theorists such as Dagger, Spragens, and Galston are so concerned to avoid in their own normative accounts of citizenship. They claim to have identified the content of good citizenship, and the beliefs and behaviors necessary for democratic self-government, but they refuse to frame the rational capacities, practical activities, and personal dispositions that are *constitutive* of "good citizenship" as being in themselves the content of the "good life" because the liberal state is supposed remain neutral. But what if there is no real difference?

DOI: 10.4324/9781032686059-5

Spragens, echoing Galston, argues that "it cannot properly and legitimately be a purpose of a liberal regime to produce 'good people' in a specific and comprehensive sense."[1] In other words, political theorists refuse to admit that good small-d democrats are also good humans, but why should this be the case if we believe that republican self-government within a liberal democracy is the best system of government? More to the point, why should public schools refuse to produce "good humans," that is, endorse a democratic way of life as the "good life," when Christian Nationalists are already producing their own "good Christians" who believe that American society should reflect their political and religious worldview? Christian Nationalists are already doing what the liberal state is supposed to refrain from and threatening liberal democracy itself and everyone's quality of life in the process.

Does this make an instrumental rationale for a normative "vision of good citizenship" the strongest argument? Should public schools promote the beliefs and behaviors of liberal democracy simply as a counter-offensive to the antidemocratic beliefs and behaviors of Christian Nationalism? Is preserving liberal democracy the strongest rationale for endorsing a normative civic education? Or is an intrinsic rationale more convincing? If, as liberals such as Galston have argued, the capacities, activities, and dispositions necessary for democratic self-government constitute a *de facto* way of life; and if, as republicans such as Dagger have argued, a vision of the "good life" is implied in normative conceptions of citizenship, then the instrumental argument that public schools could justify endorsing a "vision of good citizenship" simply because it would preserve liberal democracy should be as untenable as an Aristotelian justification that "good citizenship" is the means to the "good life." In other words, if the liberal state is expected to be neutral on the "good life," and is unwilling to equate political participation with the "good life," then how can it promote a *de facto* way of life simply for the purpose of civic education? If a liberal democracy is not willing to declare a democratic way of life the "good life," then how can it justify a normative "vision of good citizenship" as a means to preserve liberal democracy?

Republican theorists who promote civic virtue and rational autonomy on such instrumental grounds do not connect these characteristics to the "good life," which leads political theorist Paul Weithman to label their approach "political republicanism" in contrast to "perfectionist republicanism." He argues that "the problem with presenting the civic virtues as virtues in the weaker [instrumental] sense is that it makes our motive to cultivate and sustain them too heavily dependent upon our identification with our citizenship," and as a result "political republicanism does not adequately secure the conditions of its own success."[2] Weithman contends that if civic virtues are only good because of their relationship to citizenship and if individuals are expected to embrace them simply because that is what "good citizens" do, then many people will not sufficiently value them. The substance of good citizenship cannot be justified as a means to an end if the end is "good citizenship." What if students do not care about their civic obligations or choose, as is their prerogative in a liberal democracy, to abstain from political participation?

What is needed is an intrinsic rationale for promoting a normative civic education. People are unlikely to embrace a "vision of good citizenship" if it is framed narrowly as applicable solely to the role of citizen. Public schools should offer a compelling "vision of good citizenship" that has intrinsic worth, but that predisposes individuals to an active civic life. In other words, political participation is *not* the "good life"; the beliefs and behaviors necessary for political participation, a general democratic way of life, *is* the "good life." Republican civic virtue and the values of liberal democracy are intrinsically valuable for the individual and society, even if never directly applied to the political process. A democratic way of life is more than elections, it is a way of acting and thinking in the world, which takes place in the home, at work, and in the public sphere. Promoting a democratic way of life is not simply a means to promote the health of democracy, it is an end itself as a desirable way to live, think, and interact with others. In this sense, the rise of Christian Nationalism threatens so much more than the political system. It threatens a specific way of life for individuals and society outside the context of politics. For this reason, public schools should unapologetically promote a "vision of good citizenship" that prepares individuals to live a democratic way of life, as the "good life."

Thus far, political theorists have been unwilling to concede that the endorsement and cultivation of the capacities, activities, and dispositions of "good citizenship" in a democracy may be barely distinguishable from a vision of the "good life" more comprehensively. Weithman's main contribution to this debate is the insight that a perfectionist rationale that insists "better" people will make "better" citizens is more compelling than an instrumental argument that individuals must act more virtuously in their role as citizen than they do in their private life. Weithman insists that it is an error to argue that a particular virtue is a virtue because of its connection to politics if that same virtue has application to other contexts. In other words, just because a capacity to deliberate rationally is good for citizenship does not mean that the reason it is good is because it is good for citizenship—it could also be good in a more comprehensive sense.

Weithman insists that only a perfectionist republicanism "values and promotes civic virtues as genuine excellences of character."[3] His main argument is that citizens will be more likely to embrace a conception of civic virtue that is framed broadly as virtue in-itself. Expanding the line of thought, I argue that a normative "vision of good citizenship" must be promoted as a "vision of the good life." A normative civic education must take a broad-based approach to the cultivation of a democratic way of life as not being solely desirable within the context of the role of citizen or justified merely as a means to preserve liberal democracy. The substance of the normative civic education promoted by liberal and republican theorists alike is, as Weithman insists, valuable and applicable beyond the realm of politics and the role of citizen.

The strength and attraction of a perfectionist rationale are that it endorses a "vision of good citizenship" as a "vision of the good life" without coercing acceptance. I argue, counter-intuitively, that a liberal democracy can "get more for less" regarding its own self-preservation by endorsing a normative civic education on perfectionist grounds that is conducive to active political participation but not justified for that singular purpose. Weithman's "perfectionist republicanism" can promote "good citizenship as an element of a good human life"[4] without having to declare the "good life" as one devoted to politics. The rationale for promoting rational autonomy and civic virtue would not be made on instrumental grounds as necessary to preserve liberal democracy, but instead on perfectionist grounds as the capacities, activities, and dispositions of a democratic way of life. Such a normative civic education may not be significantly different from the views expressed by theorists such as Dagger and Spragens, but it would be labeled for what it is: a "vision of good citizenship" that promotes a "vision of the good life."

Weithman's contention that a perfectionist approach is necessary for individuals to positively embrace, or at a minimum acquiesce to, a "vision of good citizenship" identifies the main deficiency with instrumental justifications for a normative civic education. Despite the desire of theorists such as Sandel, the role of citizen will simply not dominate an individual's identity in a liberal society. Yet the "vision of good citizenship" that a liberal democracy promotes through its public schools as a "vision of the good life" can be conducive to the production of citizens who possess rational autonomy and civic virtue. It is not sufficient to identify what type of citizen will make a liberal democracy viable long term. To be effective, the government within a liberal democracy must consider on what grounds a "vision of good citizenship" will be accepted by the public and embraced by the individual.

A perfectionist rationale is stronger because a democratic way of life cannot be legislated or coerced; it can only be promoted and willfully embraced. People cannot be required by law to exercise civic virtue, but they can choose to be virtuous in general and are likelier to do so if they consider virtue an intrinsic end-in-itself. A normative civic education that aims to promote rational autonomy and civic virtue cannot have as its objective to accept citizens "as they are" but must instead seek to cultivate citizens "as they ought to be," which requires a positive conception of freedom and perfectionist "vision of good citizenship" that ennobles the individual beyond the role of citizen. A liberal democracy can succeed in revitalizing and preserving itself by equating a democratic way of life with the "good life," and promoting a normative "vision of good citizenship" that cultivates rational autonomy and civic virtue on perfectionist grounds that encourages the individual to embrace democracy for its own sake. Not long ago, this argument would have been deemed a brazen and unjustified departure from the "neutrality" of liberal democracy. A reckoning with contemporary conservative critics may produce a sobering acceptance that refusing to embrace a normative civic education will not preserve liberal democracy's neutrality but forfeit liberal democracy altogether.

Revolutionary and Illiberal Conservatism

Christian Nationalists, whether they are politicians or parents, are convinced that vast swaths of American society are controlled by liberals who use their positions of power to promote a progressive worldview that is hostile to conservative Christianity. Even though conservative Christians clearly control plenty of institutions themselves, such as private schools, churches, businesses, non-profits, and media, through which they can spread their values, they increasingly insist that public tax dollars should help fund the promotion of their worldview (private school vouchers) or that they should control public institutions (government, public schools). In other words, Christian Nationalists have diagnosed a problem, as they see it, and formulated a solution. Liberals control society, and conservatives must take control themselves.

As Perry and Whitehead state in *Taking America Back for God*, "it does not even matter whether the United States *is* or *ever was* a Christian nation. What matters is that a significant number of Americans *believe* that it is."[5] Likewise, it does not matter whether conservative claims about liberal control over society are true. What matters is that they are acting on their belief that it is true. Thus far, especially in the context of public education, Christian Nationalists have been on the offensive, while those opposed to them have stood on the sidelines denouncing their actions without any concrete plan to fight back. If the current trend continues, then it is likely that the Christian Nationalists will prevail. We know how they will win because they have a model and playbook: Viktor Orban's Hungary.

Rod Dreher, an influential conservative Christian voice on the far-right, views Ron DeSantis as an American Viktor Orban, the prime minister of Hungary who has openly promoted "illiberalism" as the solution to political debates between conservatives and progressives. Orban has slowly undermined democracy in Hungary by rigging elections, controlling the media and education system, and undermining the normal checks and balances that exist between the executive, legislative, and judicial branches. Dreher, summarizing why Orban has been successful in Hungary and why DeSantis is right to emulate him, writes:

> [W]e conservatives are still operating on an outdated classical-liberal model of governance, in which the private sector, as well as parts of the public sector (education), should be left alone . . . but what happens when the old-school liberals have been replaced by woke Jacobins?[6]

Dreher is speaking directly to the neutrality of the liberal state discussed by scholars such as Sandel. His point is that conservatives are losing because they are still assuming that the government should remain neutral. Orban, and now DeSantis, claims Dreher, are correct to use government power to assert conservative control over society to promote a conservative Christian worldview. Dreher believes that progressives have already abandoned neutrality and are using the liberal state to dominate conservative Christians. For this reason, he endorses a conservative counter-offensive, writing:

> What you cannot do is simply sit back and whine about how unfair they [progressives] are; or keep hoping that if you continue to point out how they have abandoned old-fashioned liberalism, they will turn back. They won't. They really hate us [conservatives] and what we stand for, and nothing is going to change that.[7]

I argue that Christian Nationalists, mistakenly believing that they are being oppressed by progressives, have gone on the offensive and now threaten to *actually* oppress their political rivals. It is the Christian Nationalists who have openly abandoned any allegiance to liberal neutrality, and it is the defenders of liberal democracy who must quickly realize that no amount of public criticism leveled at Christian Nationalists will cause them to moderate their political agenda. Conservatives such as Dreher believe that the illiberalism of Orban's Hungary is a desirable ideal for Republican politicians like DeSantis to strive toward. Even though Hungary is an illiberal democracy characterized by one-party rule, it has been embraced by Republican organizations like CPAC and media personalities like Tucker Carlson, once the most-watched news anchor on cable television, as a model for the future of the United States. Will the politicians and parents who believe in free speech, fair elections, and public schools that prepare students for participation in a diverse, pluralistic society organize and halt the advance of Christian Nationalism before it is too late?

Another example of the evolution taking place on the far-right is an article by John Daniel Davidson, writing for the influential conservative website *The Federalist*, who proposes that conservatives abandon the label "conservative" because their movement has failed to conserve traditional values and society. He insists that conservatives "should stop thinking of themselves as conservatives (much less as Republicans) and start thinking of themselves as radicals, restorationists, and counterrevolutionaries."[8] Davidson describes the political and electoral version of the educational battle being waged by Hillsdale College, Ron DeSantis, and Dan Patrick. He writes:

> [I]f conservatives want to save the country they are going to have to rebuild and in a sense re-found it. . . . The government will have to become, in the hands of conservatives, an instrument of renewal in American life—and in some cases, a blunt instrument indeed.[9]

Davidson summarizes much of what has transpired at school board meetings across America when he argues:

> Conservatives need to get comfortable saying . . . that Drag Queen Story Hour should be outlawed; that parents who take their kids to drag shows should be arrested and charged with child abuse; that doctors who perform

so-called "gender-affirming" interventions should be thrown in prison and have their medical licenses revoked; and that teachers who expose their students to sexually explicit material should not just be fired but be criminally prosecuted.[10]

In recent years, many Christian Nationalists have run for school board positions on the exact issues that Davidson highlights, and many will continue to do so. How will Americans, regardless of their religion, race, or political party, who believe in liberal democracy, respond to this authoritarian threat?

Echoing the sentiments of Dreher and Davidson, the political scientist Patrick Deneen, writing in *Regime Change*, promotes the abandonment of liberalism in favor of a post-liberal conservatism led by conservative elites. Deneen, much like Dreher, sees the power of liberals as an existential threat. He insists that the current liberal elite, which has a commitment to progressive values, represents a "new form of tyranny, apparently paradoxical: an illiberal liberalism that demands and is willing to exert power without any internal limit."[11] When Christian Nationalists successfully ban books from public school libraries, or attempt to prevent the peaceful transfer of power after a free and fair election, it is difficult to take seriously the argument that progressives are the source of illiberalism in American society.

Ultimately, Deneen embraces replacing one elite with another, stating:

> [A]n elite can and should be a defender of the cultural traditions that are mostly a development of bottom-up practices—[this] points to how democracy and a proper aristocracy are not contradictory, but, in fact, ought to be mutually supportive and beneficial.[12]

The "proper" elite, according to Deneen, would possess the "correct" cultural traditions and exercise government power to preserve and impose those traditions on society. Presumably, Deneen agrees with Dreher that today's progressives are "woke Jacobins," and what is needed are Davidson's "restorationists" or "counter-revolutionaries." In other words, a Christian Nationalist vanguard willing to take sides and use the power of the state to impose a conservative Christian worldview on society. Far from being a hypothetical academic discussion, these ideas are clearly already motivating the actions of politicians like Dan Patrick, Ron DeSantis, and Donald Trump. Not only does this illiberal mindset pose a threat to public schools, but public schools also have a role to play in defending liberal democracy.

Minority Tyranny and Liberal Democracy

As previously discussed, plenty of intellectual and political evidence exists demonstrating that Christian Nationalists are willing to abandon liberal democracy if it provides an equal playing field for political and religious values that contradict their own. For this reason, it can be challenging for educators to promote liberal democracy in public schools because the defense of small-d democracy is perceived by Christian Nationalists as a partisan effort to promote a big-D Democratic agenda. However, the values of the American republic are not partisan, and attempts to frame the expansion of voting rights or prevention of book bans as "wins" for Democrats only serves to exacerbate the illiberal threat to our shared democratic way of life. Once either side views a "win" for democracy as a "win" for Democrats, then the entire republic is threatened.

This reality is one reason why an instrumental rationale for endorsing a normative civic education is problematic and highlights the strength of an intrinsic, or perfectionist, rationale. An intrinsic approach allows the framing of the conversation to shift from "what is good for democracy is also good for Democrats" to "what is good for democracy is also good for human beings." The broader argument in favor of a normative civic education must be perceived as nonpartisan and motivated by what is good for people, not as a partisan effort that advances the values of Democrats. A normative civic education must promote a democratic way of life not just on instrumental grounds as necessary to preserve democracy but also on perfectionist grounds as beneficial for individuals and society. The rise of Christian Nationalism threatens more than the balance of power within government or the health of liberal democracy; it threatens everyone's quality of life. In other words, confronting authoritarianism is about saving not just the American republic but also the American people.

The necessary shift in civic consciousness is for policymakers, administrators, educators, and parents to publicly own the fact that a democratic way of life, characterized by democratic beliefs and behaviors, is the "good life." If someone disagrees, then they are against liberal democracy, which makes their views an authoritarian threat not only to liberal democracy's political institutions and processes but also to society more broadly. In the United States, individuals are free to adopt a wide range of political identities from anarchist to theocrat, but they are not free to prevent public schools from openly promoting liberal democracy as the best form of government or best way to live. Individuals who do not share a commitment to liberal democracy and a democratic way of life are entitled to their beliefs, but their opinions need not be taken seriously by those charged with maintaining the public school system. Furthermore, the defenders of liberal democracy, having taken sides, must forcefully and publicly rebuke illiberal and authoritarian demands.

Assuming the threat of Christian Nationalism persists, public schools must equip students to defend liberal democracy from illiberalism and even promote the further democratization of American politics and society. When students learn about liberal democracy, especially their own, they should grapple with and examine the ways in which their own political system may be undemocratic. Civic educators should also facilitate the identification and formulation of reform proposals that would enhance liberal democracy. The present Christian Nationalist threat to liberal democracy makes such a normative civic education imperative in the short term. Christian Nationalists are currently attempting to orchestrate what James Madison dismissed as antithetical to the American republic: minority tyranny. They are outnumbered, which is why they are willing to abandon liberal democracy in favor of illiberal alternatives. They believe that they are in possession of objective truth and a divine mandate and therefore justified in silencing others.

Whereas Madison assumed that diversity (of factions) would prevent tyranny, the existence of diversity has hastened the arrival of tyranny from those who oppose it. As previously discussed, the Unites States is a republic based on constitutional design features that aim to create majority rule with minority rights, which required the inclusion of what are called "counter-majoritarian" design features. The problem, identified succinctly by Steven Levitsky and Daniel Ziblatt in *Tyranny of the Minority*, is that "rules designed to fetter majorities may allow partisan minorities to *consistently* thwart and even *rule over* majorities."[13] Evidence of this tendency to empower minority factions includes the impact of the Electoral College, partisan gerrymandering, and the filibuster (to name a few). At the state and national levels, Christian Nationalist minorities have leveraged this structural advantage to win elections with fewer votes and pass legislation that lacks majority support. When Democrats criticize the undemocratic nature of the political and policymaking process, Republicans are always quick to remind the public that the United States is "not a democracy, but a republic." As stated earlier, the subtext of the retort is that minority *rule*, not just minority rights or protections, is normal and justified.

From the standpoint of civic education, the defense of minority rule is a dangerous idea and poses an instructional challenge. While counter-majoritarianism is an important feature of constitutional design in the United States, it remains the case that "counter-majoritarian institutions that thwart electoral and legislative majorities are often associated with authoritarianism, not liberal democracy."[14] However, if a teacher aims to accurately describe the malfunctions of American politics that betray the ideals of liberal democracy, they are accused of having an agenda or politicizing the curriculum. The problem, as Levitsky and Ziblatt explain, is that "only in the twenty-first century has counter-majoritarianism taken on a *partisan* cast—that is, regularly benefiting one party over another in national politics."[15] The fact that counter-majoritarianism now benefits one party over the other, almost exclusively, makes it difficult for teachers to criticize these constitutional or procedural design flaws.

For example, in the past, there was bi-partisan opposition to, or at least acknowledgment of, the undemocratic nature of the Electoral College. As a high school social studies teacher, I witnessed firsthand the shift in public attitude in my conservative suburb about the Electoral College after the 2016 election. Classroom instruction about the Electoral College that was not considered problematic or biased in 2015 was now seen as "anti-Trump" or evidence of a liberal agenda. Likewise, in the recent past, disapproval of partisan gerrymandering was shared by Republicans and Democrats. Now, a teacher may be accused of "indoctrination" for introducing students to the harmful impact that the practice has on policymaking and elections. Why? Because fairer maps would likely reduce Republican majorities to the benefit of Democrats. Concern about the counter-majoritarian features of the American political system that threaten the health of liberal democracy can be dismissed by Republicans as the evidence of partisanship even though such concerns can be based on objective criteria and a nonpartisan rationale. What is a civic educator to do?

If American public schools must remain silent about the counter-majoritarianism that threatens to undermine liberal democracy, then the next generation will not be equipped to defend or reform it. Civic education has a direct role to play in identifying the problems posed by the threat of minority tyranny and proposing solutions. It is crucial that civic educators be able to critique American constitutional design and electoral and policymaking processes without being accused of having a partisan or ideological agenda. A meaningful civic education cannot be provided to students if what is good or desirable for liberal democracy can be dismissed as what is good for liberal Democrats. The classroom must be a place where critical analysis and normative evaluation are permitted and encouraged. Furthermore, a normative civic education that promotes a "vision of good citizenship" must go beyond instruction about the design and workings of governmental institutions. It must include a reintegration of moral and character education.

Civic Reformation

As noted earlier, Christian Nationalists will gladly fill the moral vacuum created by a "neutral" liberal state that refuses to promote specific values. In recent decades, the tendency of American public schools to increasingly avoid taking sides on normative questions or controversial topics has coincided with a significant decline in both liberal mainline Protestantism and church attendance (in general). In other words, far less people, specifically children, are receiving any consistent exposure to formalized moral and ethical instruction; while at the same time, those who do attend Christian churches on a regular basis are more likely to attend conservative evangelical or non-denominational churches steeped in Christian Nationalism. As David Brooks' writing in *The Atlantic* argues:

> If you put people in a moral vacuum, they will seek to fill it with the closest thing at hand. Over the past several years, people have sought to fill the moral vacuum with politics and tribalism. American society has become hyper-politicized.[16]

Over the last decade, the moral vacuum has been filled with an aggressive Christian Nationalism on the right that seeks to "save America," and a progressive commitment on the left to what Yascha Mounk terms the "identity synthesis," which is an ideology committed to overcoming persistent injustices based on categories like gender, sexual orientation, and race. The "identity synthesis" can be understood as a different label for what conservatives deride as "woke." Mounk, in *The Identity Trap*, describes the "identity synthesis" as a trap that leads to the abandonment of the universal values at the heart of historical liberalism. He writes that "far-right ideologies are so dangerous because they discourage people from widening their circle of sympathy"[17] and expresses concern that the unintended consequence of placing too much emphasis on identity is that it will become "harder for people to broaden their allegiances beyond a particular identity in a way that can sustain stability, solidarity, and social justice."[18] Whether there is any truth to the claim by Christian Nationalists that public schools promote a "woke" agenda, the perception and belief that public schools are doing so have arguably fueled the aggressive attack on the civic mission of public schools to educate every student for participation in a diverse, pluralistic society.

While Mounk's concerns about the "illiberal" nature of some aspects of the "identity synthesis" can seem misplaced given the larger threat posed by the rise of Christian Nationalism, his point that a wholesale embrace of the "identity synthesis" would be as incompatible with liberal democracy as Christian Nationalism is well taken. He writes, "instead of encouraging citizens of diverse communities to reconceptualize themselves as part of a broader whole, progressive separatism encourages them to see each other as members of mutually irreconcilable groups."[19] In the end, he responds to progressive claims that liberalism cannot overcome historical injustices by insisting that "the best hope to keep making ... progress lies not in abandoning liberalism but in redoubling our efforts to live up to its animating ideals."[20] He, like Levitsky and Ziblatt, believes that the answer to both progressive and conservative critiques of liberal democracy is to stay the course. In doing so, American public schools have a crucial role to play.

Civic education can be the site and driver of a civic reformation that equips the next generation of Americans to preserve and gradually perfect liberal democracy. Again, a normative civic education that promotes a "vision of good citizenship" must have the aim of cultivating not good Christians or progressives, but good *humans*. This will require moral formation through a reintegration of character education within civic education to cultivate the beliefs and behaviors characteristic of living a democratic way of life. According to Brooks, "morally formative institutions hold up a set of ideals. They provide practical pathways toward a meaningful existence: *Here's how you can dedicate your life to serving the poor, or protecting the nation, or loving your neighbor.*"[21] In the absence of moral formation elsewhere, and in the face of an authoritarian Christian Nationalism speaking the language of moral formation, it is imperative that American public schools start to fill the moral vacuum by promoting the ideals of liberal democracy as a path to being a good human and cultivating a humane society.

A normative civic education that rejects the authoritarianism of Christian Nationalism and avoids the excesses of the progressive "identity synthesis" to focus on universal values of equality can serve to bridge the divide between hostile political tribes. A civic reformation that doubles down on democracy and recommits to liberalism would reject inherited thought from the recent past that limits liberal democracy to the status of a "neutral" or "minimal" state. The meaning of liberalism is not solely defined by libertarians. A renewed dialogue with the American Founders, not their modern-day "originalist" interpreters, would allow a return to republican principles that would enhance and strengthen liberal democracy. Brooks writes:

> America's Founding Fathers studied the history of democracies going back to ancient Greece. They drew the lesson that democracies can be quite fragile. When private virtue fails, the constitutional order crumbles. After decades without much in the way of moral formation, America became a place where more than 74 million people looked at Donald Trump's morality and saw presidential timber.[22]

Clearly, constitutional literacy and character education are needed, and a normative civic education can provide it. The crucial point, however, is that civic educators be permitted to teach the values of liberal democracy. The promotion of constitutional reforms that would negatively impact Republicans, but positively enhance liberal democracy, is not evidence of a partisan agenda. The cultivation of democratic character traits and behaviors, the opposite of which may be exhibited by a specific politician, is not indoctrination.

Civic education is at a crossroads. The civic mission of America's public schools, and the values of liberal democracy itself, are threatened by the rise of Christian Nationalism. Far from being a fringe ideology, Christian Nationalism is now the political worldview that informs the policy agenda of elected officials from local school board trustees to the Speaker of the U.S. House of Representatives. Christian Nationalists reject the notion that the United States is a multicultural, religiously pluralistic society. They believe that the Unites States was founded as a "Christian nation" and that conservative Christians have a right and duty to control government and promote their worldview through public policy. Christian Nationalists believe so strongly in their right and duty to rule that they now increasingly abandon liberal democracy itself in their pursuit of power.

American public schools have become a central battleground in the conflict over America's identity and future. Seeking to wrest control from those they claim are using public schools to indoctrinate students with a progressive worldview that is hostile to conservative Christianity, Christian Nationalists have aggressively attacked public education in the hopes of either taking control themselves or discrediting public schools with the aim of increasing support for private school vouchers. Local school boards have banned books and passed policies creating hostile learning environments for LGBTQ+ students. State legislatures have passed legislation banning specific instructional resources, limiting free speech, and undermining the separation of church and state. Nationally, Christian Nationalism is a worldview that inspires members of the U.S. Supreme Court, leaders within Congress, and presidential candidates. Conservative intellectuals enthusiastically applaud and encourage the rise of Christian Nationalism as a compelling and unifying path to electoral success.

While much has been written about Christian Nationalism from a religious, sociological, and political perspective, I have tried to illuminate the role that public schools can play in addressing the threat posed by Christian Nationalism to liberal democracy and a democratic way of life. Liberal democracy must abandon its "neutrality," and public schools must ignore the false claims that they indoctrinate students with a progressive worldview. What is needed, now more than ever, is a normative civic education that unapologetically promotes a "vision of good citizenship" that cultivates rational autonomy and civic virtue as intrinsic goods that enable individuals to live fulfilling lives. A liberal democracy like the United States should no longer hesitate to endorse a democratic way of life as the "good life" and the small-d democratic citizen as a "good human." While the capacities, activities, and dispositions of a democratic way of life are certainly useful instrumentally to preserve liberal democracy, they are also intrinsically valuable for human beings to live a good life. In responding to the threat posed by Christian Nationalism, policymakers, administrators, and educators in public schools must take sides and commit to cultivating good humans equipped with the beliefs and behaviors necessary to confront authoritarianism.

The classroom should be a place of ethical exploration and intellectual curiosity. The curriculum should enable and encourage students to develop agency, empathy, and solidarity. While it may be wrong for a White student to be told that they *must* feel a sense of guilt about the history of white supremacy in the United States, it is entirely reasonable, and even admirable, for them to do so on their own. The state of Texas banned the use of *The 1619 Project* because it might make White students feel discomfort or guilt. Why shouldn't Americans feel guilt about the past? I assume that Germans feel guilt about the Holocaust when they learn about it in school. Why do Christian Nationalists object so forcefully to the idea that students may feel guilt about events in America's past? Why is it legal for students in Texas to read excerpts from Adolf Hitler's *Mein Kampf* and condemn the Final Solution, but illegal to read *The 1619 Project* and condemn the institution of slavery? Why do Christian Nationalists insist that it is appropriate for students to feel pride about America's past but not shame? If we truly are the inheritors of the past, then we should feel a variety of emotions about it. If American students are prevented from learning about the complexity of the past or denied the opportunity to read a book that allows them to see the world through someone else's eyes, then they will lack the wisdom and imagination to navigate their own lives or pass a more humane society on to future generations.

The United States has been, and continues to be, one of the greatest experiments in the history of the world. Learning about the good, bad, and ugly of its past need not diminish the pride and hope that Americans feel. Through all its imperfections, the American republic has stood for individual freedom and equal opportunity. Each generation has had the chance to redefine those concepts for themselves. The chance for today's youth to do the same is under threat by the rise of Christian Nationalism. Liberal democracy can be preserved. If provided with a meaningful civic education, the next generation can have the same opportunity to gradually perfect the Union. Civic education is at a crossroads. The liberal promise of the American republic can endure, only if we teach it.

Notes

1 Thomas Spragens, *Civic Liberalism* (Lanham: Rowman and Littlefield, 1999), 35.
2 Paul Weithman, "Political Republicanism and Perfectionist Republicanism," *The Review of Politics* 66, no. 2 (2004): 286.
3 Ibid., 287.
4 Ibid., 307.
5 Andrew L. Whitehead and Samuel L. Perry, *Taking America Back for God: Christian Nationalism in the United States* (New York: Oxford University Press, 2020), 4.
6 Rod Dreher, "DeSantis: A Conservative Living in the Real World," *The American Conservative*, January 27, 2023.
7 Ibid.
8 John Daniel Davidson, "We Need to Stop Calling Ourselves Conservatives," *The Federalist*, October 20, 2022.
9 Ibid.
10 Ibid.
11 Patrick J. Deneen, *Regime Change: Toward a Postliberal Future* (London: Swift Press, 2023), 52.
12 Ibid., 125.
13 Steven Levitsky and Daniel Ziblatt, *The Tyranny of the Minority* (New York: Crown, 2023), 142.
14 Ibid., 143.
15 Ibid., 169.
16 David Brooks, "How America Got Mean," *The Atlantic*, August 14, 2023.
17 Yascha Mounk, *The Identity Trap: A Story of Ideas and Power in Our Time* (New York: Penguin Press, 2023), 14.
18 Ibid.
19 Ibid., 193.
20 Ibid., 251.
21 Brooks, "How America Got Mean."
22 Ibid.

Index

The 1619 Project 54, 55, 74

Abbott, Greg 24, 27, 44
American Founding 5, 13–18, 21, 54–55
Anti-Defamation League 49
Aristotle 15, 17, 21, 62
The Atlantic (Brooks) 71
autonomy: individual 3, 31–35, 37, 40, 48; rational 32–37, 63

Berlin, Isaiah 20, 34–35
Berman, Ari 52
big-D Democratic agenda 69
Brooks, David 71–73

capitalism, socialist threat to 59
Carlson, Tucker 67
Ceaser, James 17–19
character education 36, 38, 71–73
The Christendom Curriculum 55–56
Christianity 36, 45, 54, 55, 57
Christian Nationalism 1, 3, 9, 20, 30, 44, 62, 64, 69; and American identity 6–7; as authoritarian ideology 19, 72–73; defined 5; fringe ideology 73; ideology and private school/homeschool 11; infiltrating suburban Houston 40–43; laboratories of 58–60; liberal democracy and 62, 72; and public schools 5–7; threat of 69, 72–75
Christian Nationalist 3, 19, 30, 31, 33, 35, 38, 39–40, 42, 58, 63, 66–68, 70; activists and lawmakers 54; agenda 56, 59; anti-mask 27–28; critics of public education 56; crusade 43; in "Culture War" theatrics 45; defined 11; forcing their values on public schools 6–7, 9–10, 20; homeschool curriculum 55; illiberal worldview on society 59; instructional resources 56; minorities 70; objections to colleges and universities 58; parents 38–39; and pluralism 6; political and religious worldview 62; progressive "indoctrination" on college campuses 59; propaganda 42; public school system 59; rejection of American public schools 58; rhetoric and conservative bias 40, 59; threats 37; worldview 41, 49, 56
civic consciousness 69
civic duty 22–25
civic liberalism 32, 32
Civic Liberalism (Spragens) 32
civic reformation 71–75
"civic republican" approach to civic education 37
Civic Republicanism and Civic Education (Peterson) 37
civic virtue 17, 18, 20–22, 32–37, 40, 60, 62–65
Civic Virtues (Dagger) 30
Civil War 50
Civitas Institute 58

The Common Good (Reich) 40
conservatism 54; illiberal
 conservatism 66–68;
 revolutionary conservatism
 66–68
conservative bias 10–11, 57, 58
conservative ideologues 59
counter-majoritarianism 70–71
COVID-19 pandemic 16, 20; mask
 mandates 23–28
CPAC 67
Critical Race Theory (CRT) 8,
 40–41, 42–44
critical thinking 4, 7
"critic of liberalism" 30
Culture War 10, 45, 56, 59

Dagger, Richard 30–31, 32, 34–36,
 62, 63, 65
Dahl, Robert 52
Davidson, John Daniel 67–68
Davis, Jefferson 50
democracy: American 6, 10, 19,
 22, 32, 35–38; defined 13;
 democratic way of life 64–65,
 69, 72; liberal 1–3; and public
 schools 1–4; *see also* liberal
 democracy
Democracy's Discontent (Sandel)
 21, 48
Democratic Education (Gutmann) 31
Deneen, Patrick 19, 37, 68
DeSantis, Ron 59, 66–68
diversity 37–40
Dreher, Rod 66–68

educators 60–61; act as
 "Ambassadors" of liberal
 democracy 61; on
 beliefs and behaviors of
 liberal democracy 61; on
 conservative Christian bias
 60; professionalism/expertise/
 integrity 61
Electoral College 1, 14, 70
equity 37–40
Everytown for Gun Safety 53
Executive Order GA-38 24

*The Flag and the Cross: White
 Christian Nationalism and the
 Threat to American Democracy*
 (Perry and Gorski) 6, 27
Floyd, George 41, 54
Fund, John 53

Galston, William 30, 31, 32, 33, 36,
 62, 63
George III, King of Great Britain 16
Girl Scouts of America 36
*Give Us the Ballot: The Modern
 Struggle for Voting Rights in
 America* (Berman) 52–53
good citizenship 1–2, 36, 62–65;
 vision of good citizenship 1–2,
 10, 19, 22, 24, 28, 60, 62–65,
 71–72, 74
good life 30–36, 62–65
Gorski, Philip 6–7, 27
Great Depression 17
Gutmann, Amy 30, 31–32, 36

HB 3979 bill 5–6
"health care death panels" 41
Heritage Classical Academy,
 Houston 56–57
higher education: institutions of
 liberal indoctrination 58; purpose
 of 58
Hillsdale College, Michigan 56–57,
 58, 67
Hitler, Adolf 74
Hixenbaugh, Mike 44
How Democracies Die (Levitsky and
 Ziblatt) 9
Hurricane Harvey 53

identity synthesis 71–73
The Identity Trap (Mounk) 72
illiberal conservatism 66–68
illiberalism 3, 66, 68
immigrant caravans 41
inclusion 37–40
individual autonomy 3, 31–35, 37,
 40, 48
individualism 16–17, 18, 19, 20, 21,
 25, 60

Jefferson, Thomas 15–16, 35
Jones, Alex 53

King, Martin Luther, Jr. 43
Krause, Matt 44

laboratories of Christian Nationalism 58–60
Leadership Congress 59
Lee, Mike 14
Levitsky, Steven 9, 70, 72
LGBTQ+: community 6–7, 38–39, 56, 58; equality 38, 39; inclusion 33, 41; individuals 38; rights 4, 38, 39; students 74; teachers 56
liberal democracy 1–3, 30, 60–62, 74–75; defined 11; and minority tyranny 68–71; neutrality of 19, 48–51, 60, 65; as partisan issue 7–11; and public school system 60; requires republican civic virtue 20–22; United States 19; values of 60, 64
liberal individualism 18–19
liberalism 14–16, 32, 73; abandonment of 68; and American political system 17; critics of 20; individual rights 19, 21; personal freedom 19, 21; political theorists on 19
Liberal Purposes (Galston) 31
Lincoln, Abraham 50
Locke, John 15, 35

Madison, James 13–14, 15, 70
Marx, Karl 43
militia movement 60
minority tyranny 68–71
Moms Demand Action 53
Mounk, Yascha 71–72

negative freedom 20, 21, 23; mask mandates 23–24
neutrality of liberal democracy 19, 48–51, 60, 65
The New York Times Magazine 54
No Place for Hate program 38, 49

normative civic education 30–32, 62–65, 69, 71–74

Obama, Barack 7–8
On Democracy (Dahl) 52
Orban, Viktor 66–67
Orwell, George 59

parental rights 35, 39, 41, 43
parental rights groups 3–4, 7
partisan neutrality 25–28
Patrick, Dan 58, 59, 67, 68
Patriot Academy 59–60; Biblical, Historical, and Constitutional principles 59; Constitutional Defense Center 59; Leadership Congress 59
Pence, Mike 1
A People's History of the United States (Zinn) 54
perfectionist rationale 65, 69; for civic education 62–65
perfectionist republicanism 63, 64, 65
Perry, Samuel L. 5–7, 27, 66
Peterson, Andrew 37
political education: *vs.* civic education 18; defined 18
political participation 9, 21–22, 31, 35–36, 62–65
political republicanism 63
political science 17
political theory 17–20; and American public schools challenges 22–23
positive freedom 20, 24
post-liberal conservatism 68
private school/homeschool 11
public education system 58
public health 22–25
public schools 7, 24, 30, 35, 60, 62, 71–73; and charges of indoctrination 2, 6–7, 9; Christian Nationalist threat to 5–7, 57; and civic education 1–2, 17, 19; LGBTQ+ agenda in 38; and liberal democracy 60; and

parental rights 4; promotion of democracy 1–4, 36–37, 49

rational autonomy 32–37, 63
rational deliberation 34
Regime Change (Deneen) 68
Reich, Robert 40
religious pluralism 5, 56, 60, 73
republicanism 14–22, 32, 63; as alternative to liberalism 22
Republicanism (Viroli) 21
republican self-government 11
republican theorists 35, 37, 62–64
revolutionary conservatism 66–68
"The Role of Political Science and Political Scientists in Civic Education" (Ceaser) 18

Sandel, Michael J. 21–22, 31, 48, 62, 65, 66
Shelby County v. Holder 52
small-d democracy 69
small-d democratic citizen 62, 74
small-d democrats 63
social contract 15–16
socialism 16, 40, 41, 55, 59
Spragens, Thomas 30, 32–36, 62, 63, 65
state curriculum standards 58

Tackett, Chris 43
Tackett, Mendi 43
Taking America Back for God: Christian Nationalism in the United States (Whitehead and Perry) 5, 43, 66
teaching: both sides to picking sides 54–57; lies to teach the truth 51–53
Tea Party 7

Texas: and Christian Nationalism 43–45; exceptionalism 54; HB 3979 57; House Bill 3979 54; State Board of Education 56; TEKS (Texas's content standards) 52
Texas Education Agency 5, 44
Texas Monthly 54
Texas State Board of Education 56
Texas Tribune 59
Trump, Donald 1, 8, 51, 68; 1776 Commission 55; "Election Integrity Commission" 52, 53
truth 51–53
"Two Concepts of Liberalism" (Galston) 33
Tyranny of the Minority (Levitsky and Ziblatt) 70

Viroli, Maurizio 21–22
vision of good citizenship 1–2, 10, 19, 22, 24, 28, 60, 62–65, 71–72, 74
von Spakovky, Hans 53
Voting Rights Act 53

Weithman, Paul 63–65
West Texas A&M University 59
West Texas values 59
Whitehead, Andrew L. 5, 66
Who's Counting: How Fraudsters and Bureaucrats Put Your Vote at Risk (Fund and von Spakovky) 53

The Yellow Rose of Texas Republican Women 45

Ziblatt, Daniel 9, 70, 72
Zinn, Howard 54

For Product Safety Concerns and Information please contact our EU
representative GPSR@taylorandfrancis.com
Taylor & Francis Verlag GmbH, Kaufingerstraße 24, 80331 München, Germany

www.ingramcontent.com/pod-product-compliance
Lightning Source LLC
Chambersburg PA
CBHW071513150426
43191CB00009B/1519